Universal credit
What you need
to know

Cardiff Libraries
www.cardiff.gov.uk/libraries

Llyfrgelloedd Caerdy
www.cardiff.gov.uk/llyfrgell

ChiLd Pov

Published by Child Poverty Action Group
94 White Lion Street
London N1 9PF
Tel: 020 7837 7979
staff@cpag.org.uk
www.cpag.org.uk
© Child Poverty Action Group 2012

A CIP record for this book is available from the British Library.
ISBN: 978 1 906076 60 3

Child Poverty Action Group is a charity registered in England and Wales (registration
number 294841) and in Scotland (registration number SC039339), and is a company
limited by guarantee, registered in England (registration number 1993854). VAT number:
690 808117

Cover and typography by Devious Designs
Content management system by KonnectSoft
Typeset by David Lewis XML Associates Ltd
Printed and bound in the UK by CPI Group (UK) Ltd, Croydon CR0 4YY

Authors

The authors of this book are all welfare rights workers at CPAG in Scotland.

Alison Gillies is a welfare rights worker with the Children and Families project.

Henri Krishna is a welfare rights worker with the BME Communities project.

Judith Paterson is welfare rights co-ordinator.

Jon Shaw is a welfare rights worker with the Children and Families project.

Angela Toal is a welfare rights worker with the Benefits for Students project.

Mark Willis is a welfare rights worker with the Tax Credits and Early Years project.

Acknowledgements

The authors would like to thank David Simmons for his expert eye in checking this book, and Tim Nichols and Alison Garnham for their insight and guidance on welfare reform. Many thanks are due to Alison Key for her vigilant and thorough editing and for managing the production. Thanks are also due to Katherine Dawson for producing the index and Kathleen Armstrong for proofreading the text. We are also particularly grateful for all the hard work done by Nigel Taylor of Devious Designs and Mike Hatt of DLXML.

About Child Poverty Action Group

Child Poverty Action Group is a national charity working for the abolition of child poverty in the UK and for the improvement of the lives of low-income families.

To help achieve this goal, we have developed a high level of expertise in the welfare benefits system. We use this to support thousands of frontline advisers with our expert training and free helplines, enabling them to give families the best information and advice.

We also publish a widely used series of practitioner handbooks: our annual *Welfare Benefits and Tax Credits Handbook* (known as 'the adviser's bible') is used by Citizens Advice Bureaux, local authorities and law centres throughout the UK.

Our policy, campaigning and lobbying work builds support for policy improvements to help children living in poverty. We host the End Child Poverty campaign, a national coalition of charities, faith groups and other organisations working to hold the government to its target of beating child poverty by 2020.

If you would like to help with our campaign to end child poverty, please visit our website at www.cpag.org.uk. You can also get the latest news by following us on Facebook (www.facebook.com/cpaguk) and Twitter @CPAGUK.

Keeping up to date

Advisers can get the latest information on universal credit by booking on a CPAG training course, held in both London and Glasgow. We can also provide your workplace with in-house training. See www.cpag.org.uk/training for more information.

Our *Welfare Benefits and Tax Credits Handbook* 2012/13, published in April 2012, contains the latest information on universal credit, personal independence payment and other welfare reform measures. It also tells you all you need to know about entitlement to benefits and tax credits from April 2012.

Getting advice

Your local Citizens Advice Bureau or other advice centre can give you advice and support on benefits. See www.citizensadvice.org.uk if you live in England or Wales, or www.cas.org.uk if you live in Scotland.

CPAG has an advice line for advisers.

For advisers throughout the UK:
Telephone: 020 7833 4627, Monday to Friday 2pm to 4pm

For advisers in Scotland:
Telephone: 0141 552 0552, Monday to Friday 10am to 12pm
Email: advice@cpagscotland.org.uk

Foreword

Welcome to the first in a new series of CPAG publications, designed primarily for a non-specialist audience.

Universal credit will be phased in from October 2013 as the main working-age benefit in the UK. Its introduction and associated upheaval will come at a time when family budgets, especially those of the poorest, continue to be squeezed. As the Institute for Fiscal Studies has noted, 88 per cent of welfare benefit cuts announced by the government will be implemented after April 2012.

This crisis in family budgets will be encountered directly by claimants, and indirectly by voluntary sector workers, children's and health professionals, council officials and many others working with low-income families. Moreover, by the time universal credit is introduced, the advice services needed to respond to the new scheme will have been badly hit by local authority cuts. As a result, both claimants and practitioners who, to date, may have had only limited experience of the benefits system, will need to know how universal credit functions. It is for this broad group of people that this book has been produced.

Universal credit combines most of the support currently provided to working-age people in a single benefit. By combining in- and out-of-work benefits, it seeks to remove barriers to employment that many currently experience. In the future, claimants will be able to take up any amount of work without the disruption of losing support for a period of time as their claim for one benefit shuts down and a new one begins. Universal credit will also be calculated using real-time information about wages, rather than the lagged data on which tax credits have been based. As a result, incomes should be smoother and budgeting easier.

Universal credit has other new features. It will be assessed on a joint rather than an individual basis and, as a result, changes in the circumstances of one member of a couple could have a significant impact for the other. Nowhere will this be more acutely felt than in the area of conditionality, where one partner may be penalised for the other's failure to abide by the terms of her/his claimant commitment.

Conditionality will pinch in other ways too. For example, in contrast with tax credits, those who claim universal credit while they are in work will be required to seek an increase in their hours or a more highly paid job until a certain income threshold is reached. Claimants will be expected to look for work further away from home than at present (with a 90-minute as opposed to the current 60-minute commute being considered reasonable under the new regime), as well as sooner (once the youngest child in a family turns five as opposed to the current age of seven).

Universal credit will also usher in changes to the way that payments are made to claimants. In most circumstances, one member of the household must be elected to receive payments, and how this is then distributed within the family will become an entirely private matter. The current default option that payments are made to the main carer will end. Moreover, universal credit will be paid on a monthly rather than a fortnightly basis, a change that may impact on the ability of many on low incomes to budget effectively.

Rolling the vast majority of working-age benefits into one does have some real advantages, however, not least that most claimants should find the new system simpler to navigate and so may be able to access their full entitlements with greater ease. However, as with any means-tested benefit, complexity will remain a feature of the system, albeit concealed behind a simpler interface. In addition, a single benefit also has its risks. The IT system underpinning universal credit is sophisticated and there is a chance that it may not function effectively from the start. Individuals and families will be highly exposed if anything goes wrong with their claim and, in some cases, discretionary payments will be the only fall-back income available to them. Given this, accurate and timely advice for claimants is a critical part of making universal credit work.

Making work pay is the core objective of the government's welfare reform programme and universal credit has been designed in this context. It will stand or fall on whether it can truly encourage claimants to take up and progress in work. Under the current design, work incentives for some groups, such as lone parents and second earners, are weak. Help with childcare costs will be less than that provided under tax credits before April 2011, and this will further hinder some from being able to take up work. Likewise, families with disabled children will lose out on critical support. If universal credit cannot deliver on its promise of making work pay, it will be no less of a poverty trap for such groups than any previous system to date.

In the drive to incentivise work it must not be forgotten that our benefits system should deliver on other objectives too. It should protect us from shocks to our incomes and ensure a decent standard of living for all. Universal credit looks to address many of the deficiencies of the current benefits regime, yet it is also being introduced at the same time as the benefit cap which delinks the amount of support provided by the state from need. So, to what extent universal credit will, as the centrepiece of the new system, succeed in delivering true social security in the future remains to be seen.

Alison Garnham
Chief Executive, CPAG

Contents

Chapter 1
Introduction

This chapter covers:

1. What is universal credit?

2. The background

3. How is universal credit administered?

4. Which benefits are abolished?

5. The timetable for change

6. Other planned changes to benefits

What you need to know

- Universal credit is a new benefit for people of working age, who are in or out of work. It is planned to be introduced from October 2013.

- Universal credit will be administered by the Department for Work and Pensions, with the majority of contact with claimants expected to be online.

- The amount of your universal credit depends on your income and savings – ie, it is 'means tested'. You do not need to have paid national insurance contributions to qualify.

- Other means-tested benefits and tax credits will be abolished. Claimants will be transferred from the old system to universal credit over several years.

- Some other benefits remain outside universal credit, but are also being reformed.

- The Welfare Reform Act 2012 contains the basic provisions for universal credit. More details will be set out in future regulations.

1. What is universal credit?

Universal credit is a new social security benefit, planned to be introduced throughout Great Britain from October 2013. It will combine the current means-tested support for adults of working age and children into one benefit. All the current means-tested benefits and tax credits will be abolished. This means that, from October 2013, if you are a lone parent, sick or disabled, a carer, unemployed, or in low-paid work and need help with living expenses, including your rent or mortgage, the means-tested benefit you will claim will be universal credit.

What does this guide cover?

This guide tells you what you need to know about universal credit, including who can claim and how it will work. At the time of writing, the main structure of universal credit is in place (in the Welfare Reform Act 2012), but the details are still to be published. These will be in the form of regulations, which are expected to be issued later in 2012. However, the government has said how it intends the new system to work in many respects. We have included this information, as well as our own comment and analysis.

The basic facts you need to know are listed at the start of each chapter. Each chapter also includes what information is already settled in the law and what is still subject to change until the regulations are produced.

As universal credit is still under development, there are many questions which we cannot answer at the time of writing. We have indicated where this is the case and say what we expect is likely to happen.

How is universal credit different?

Universal credit has been heralded as setting a 'new course for the welfare state', 'a radical new approach' and 'fundamental reform'. But how different is it really? If you already know the benefits and tax credits system, many features of universal credit will be familiar to you. However, there are significant new features that are very different from the current system.

Universal credit and the current system	
Similarities	Differences
Most claimants are required to be available for and actively seeking work. There are special rules for carers, lone parents and sick or disabled people. Sick or disabled people are assessed to determine the extent to which their illness or disability affects their ability to work. Only the most severely disabled people, their carers and a baby's main carer (and some others) are exempt from the requirements aimed at getting people back into work.	There is a single payment for claimants, children and housing costs, whether you are in work or out of work. There are no rules about the number of hours you can work. As your income increases, your benefit reduces at a single rate of withdrawal. You do not need to report changes in your earnings, as there is 'real-time information' from HM Revenue and Customs.

2. The background

The starting point

In 2009, *Dynamic Benefits: towards welfare that works* was published by the Centre for Social Justice, an independent thinktank founded by Iain Duncan Smith to investigate and promote solutions to deep-rooted poverty in Britain. This report proposed a total overhaul of the benefits system, with poverty and unemployment slashed by ensuring that people had a meaningful incentive to work. It proposed replacing the current complex system of 51 different benefits and tax credits with a 'universal life credit' and 'universal work credit'. The costs of the new system would be partially offset by increased tax revenue from more people in work and, in the longer term, would save money by reducing other costs to society.

The government's case for reform

Iain Duncan Smith, as the new Secretary of State for Work and Pensions, presented the government's case for reform in the Green Paper, *21st Century Welfare*, published in July 2010. This argued that the current benefits system was too complex and did not give people the incentive to work, and asked for views on five possible options for reform.

- **A universal credit**: bringing out-of-work and in-work support together in a single system with additional amounts to reflect people's circumstances.

- **A single unified taper**: keeping most existing benefits and credits, but withdrawing benefit at one rate from people with earnings.

- **A single working-age benefit**: giving all working-age claimants the same level of out-of-work income, with separate provision for extra costs, and keeping tax credits.

- **The 'Mirrlees model'**: replacing benefits and tax credits with an integrated payment to be withdrawn through the income tax system.

- **A single benefit/negative income tax model**: replacing benefits and tax credits with payments through the tax system, keeping some benefits for people who need extra support.

It was clear that the government had already made up its mind that universal credit was its preferred option and, despite its being described as the biggest shake-up in the welfare state since its inception, there was no consultation on this specific proposal.

Universal credit proposals

The consultation on the Green Paper closed in October 2010 with 1,668 responses. A little over a month later, in November 2010, the White Paper, *Universal Credit: welfare that works*, was published. This set out the government's proposals.

- Universal credit will be an integrated benefit, replacing existing means-tested benefits and tax credits, and including additional amounts for people's circumstances.

- It will improve work incentives by scrapping complicated rules about hours and moving in and out of work.

- By allowing people to keep 35p in every pound of their earnings, it will 'make work pay'.

- No one will have a reduction in their benefits at the point when they are moved onto the new system.

What CPAG says

The government's arguments

No one will be worse off

The government has promised that no one will be worse off when universal credit is introduced. However, this is in the context of the £18 billion in welfare cuts over three years that have already begun. Even the Centre for Social Justice, of which Iain Duncan Smith was formerly chair, has criticised some aspects of the wider welfare reform plans, such as the cuts to child benefit.

If you are worse off under universal credit, the government intends to give you an additional payment, so you continue to receive the same amount in total as you were getting at the point you were transferred to universal credit. However, this transitional amount will be frozen until your universal credit reaches the same amount as your previous benefits, so in real terms you will be worse off when the other benefit rates increase each April. Furthermore, two families with very similar circumstances could receive significantly different amounts, depending on whether they claim benefit before or after universal credit is introduced. Additions for most disabled children, for example, are set to be half the amount of those for current tax credits.

What CPAG says

The government's arguments

It will be simple

The guiding principle of universal credit is its supposed simplicity. However, it is clear that much complexity remains in some key aspects, such as in the way in which earnings are treated. In essence, universal credit replaces six means-tested benefits and tax credits, but many benefits will remain outside the universal credit system. This may not seem so simple to claimants or advisers. The reform will also take place at the same time as disability living allowance is replaced by a new benefit (personal independence payment), and while local authorities and the Scottish and Welsh governments take over council tax benefit and parts of the social fund.

The Welfare Reform Act 2012

The Welfare Reform Act 2012 was passed on 8 March 2012. This lays the foundations for universal credit in the following areas:

- claims
- basic conditions
- calculation of awards
- the claimant commitment
- sanctions
- hardship payments

The Act gives the government the power to make more detailed regulations at a later date.

3. How is universal credit administered?

Universal credit will be administered by a single agency in one government department, the **Department for Work and Pensions (DWP)**. This will undergo a large scale transformation of its services and structure. The DWP currently deals with the out-of-work benefits

What CPAG says

The government's arguments

It will make work pay

Universal credit is intended to improve the incentive to work. However, there are some built-in disincentives.

- According to the DWP, 2.1 million families will see an increase in the rate at which they lose money when in work. This is because tax credits have a more generous withdrawal rate, allowing people to keep 59p in every pound of their earnings. However, because of the interaction with the housing benefit rules, it is people on relatively higher incomes or without housing costs who gained more under tax credits.

- If one partner in a couple is in work, there is little incentive for the other partner to work. This is because there is only one earnings disregard per household, so if the other partner starts work, her/his earnings will immediately affect the amount of universal credit the couple receive.

- There is inadequate support for childcare costs. Universal credit will not cover childcare costs in full and, despite rising childcare charges, there will be set limits.

- Despite tougher than ever sanctions for people who do not comply with the new work-related requirements, a steady supply of accessible, flexible jobs with living wages, parent-friendly employers and equal opportunities for people with disabilities are absent.

that will be abolished and will handle the transfer of these claims to universal credit.

HM Revenue and Customs (HMRC) is currently responsible for administering tax credits, which will also be abolished. When universal credit is introduced, HMRC will gather 'real-time information', so that payments of universal credit can be automatically adjusted as your earnings change. In practice, some parts of the tax credits infrastructure may be moved to universal credit. Child benefit will remain the responsibility of HMRC.

Local authorities currently administer housing benefit and council tax benefit, which will be abolished. Local authorities may keep some functions relating to local rents and will still be responsible for council tax support. They may also have a role in providing face-to-face support for vulnerable people claiming universal credit, as well as administering other financial provision, such as help with NHS costs and free school lunches, and possibly discretionary grants.

What CPAG says

A single agency?

In principle, a single agency delivering universal credit is welcome. Instead of having to tell the same facts to three different agencies, you will report to one department only. Currently, overpayments and underpayments of benefits are often caused by departments not communicating with each other, and this problem should be removed.

Although the government has described universal credit as a 'single integrated benefit', the amount payable will be affected by things like how many children you are responsible for and the rate of disability living allowance payable for your child. Because of this, the DWP will still need to interact with HMRC (which will continue to deal with child benefit, receipt of which is often used to prove responsibility for children) and with other sections within the DWP (which will still pay disability and carers' benefits).

Who makes the decisions?

Decisions on entitlement, amounts and sanctions will be made by a decision maker at the Department for Work and Pensions (DWP).

The administration of all the 'work-related requirements' may be contracted out to other agencies, who will act on behalf of the DWP. This is a continuation of the current situation in which private companies or public sector or voluntary agencies are paid by results to carry out the government's Work Programme. These agencies will employ personal advisers, who will set the terms of your 'claimant commitment', hold 'work-focused interviews' and require you to take particular action to prepare for or search for work. There is more information about the claimant commitment and work-related requirements in Chapter 5.

Online assessments

Most universal credit claims will be made online, with the assessment and award usually calculated automatically by a new computer system. The majority of people will be expected to communicate with the Department for Work and Pensions online – eg, in order to report any changes in their circumstances. The government envisages a role for local authorities in delivering face-to-face support for people who cannot access online services because they do not have use of a computer or a smart phone.

The new system will adjust your universal credit payments according to your earnings, which will be reported through an upgraded 'real-time' version of PAYE (Pay As You Earn). This will require every employer in the country to send data every month to HM Revenue and Customs.

There is more information about how claims will be dealt with in Chapter 3.

What CPAG says

Administration

According to the government, the successful administration of universal credit will require two 'moderate-scale' IT developments. However, this has been described by experts as 'the most complicated ever undertaken', and some people believe the current timescale is unrealistic.

More recently, the government has said that existing IT systems will be reused and updated to provide 60 per cent of what is needed for universal credit. This is scant reassurance for claimants and advisers who have good reason to have little faith in the current systems.

4. Which benefits are abolished?

Means-tested benefits and tax credits will be abolished and replaced with universal credit.

What the law says

Benefits and tax credits to be abolished

The benefits and tax credits to be abolished and replaced by universal credit are:

- income support
- income-based jobseeker's allowance
- income-related employment and support allowance
- housing benefit
- child tax credit
- working tax credit

Section 33 Welfare Reform Act 2012

The benefits listed above will be abolished for new claims to coincide with the planned introduction of universal credit in October 2013. It is

planned that no new claims for tax credits will be accepted from
April 2014.

Box A
Which benefits remain?

- attendance allowance
- bereavement allowance
- bereavement payment
- carer's allowance
- child benefit
- cold weather payments
- constant attendance allowance
- disability living allowance (to be replaced for working-age
  people by personal independence payment from April 2013)
- contributory employment and support allowance
- free school lunches
- funeral payments
- guardian's allowance
- Healthy Start vouchers
- help with health costs
- industrial injuries benefits
- contribution-based jobseeker's allowance
- maternity allowance
- maternity grant
- pension credit
- retirement pension
- school clothing grant
- statutory adoption pay
- statutory maternity pay
- statutory paternity pay
- statutory sick pay
- war disablement pension
- war widow's and widower's pension
- widowed parent's allowance
- winter fuel payment

If you are already getting one of the benefits or tax credits that will be abolished in October 2013, payments will not stop immediately. There will be a period of transfer during which you will continue to get these benefits or tax credits until you are moved onto universal credit. The process and order of moving existing claimants onto universal credit has not yet been finalised, but will be done in phases – eg, by transferring income-based jobseeker's allowance claimants first. It is intended that this process will be completed by October 2017.

Universal credit will not replace all current benefits, however, and it is not a single working-age benefit system. You will still be able to claim the benefits shown in Box A after universal credit has been introduced, although some of these are being reformed.

Council tax benefit will also be abolished, but it will not be part of universal credit. Instead, local authorities and the Scottish and Welsh governments will take it over from April 2013. Crisis loans and community care grants from the social fund are also being abolished and will be replaced by a new system to be devised and delivered by local authorities and the Scottish and Welsh governments.

There is more information about universal credit and other benefits in Chapter 8.

5. The timetable for change

You cannot claim universal credit now. The planned date for its introduction is October 2013. It is intended that the new system will be tested in pilot areas from spring 2013. The government intends that claimants will be transferred from the old benefits and tax credits system to the new universal credit system in three phases.

Box B
Proposed timetable

Spring 2013: live testing of universal credit in pilot areas.

October 2013: launch of universal credit nationwide. No new claims for:

- income support
- income-based jobseeker's allowance
- income-related employment and support allowance

If you become unemployed or unable to work from October 2013, you now claim universal credit instead of the above benefits. **Note:** you can still claim contribution-based jobseeker's allowance and contributory employment and support allowance.

You can now also claim universal credit if you are in work but are not getting any benefits or tax credits – eg, if you are in a low-paid job and you have no children, especially if you are under 25 or working fewer than 30 hours a week.

The government has said that claims for housing benefit by people of working age will be phased out by April 2014, so new claims may still be possible if you are already getting an existing benefit or tax credit and become liable for housing costs betweeen October 2013 and April 2014.

October 2013 to April 2014: Phase 1.

If you have been getting one of the above benefits, you can claim universal credit from October 2013 if you have a change of circumstances – eg, you start work or you have your first baby. The government has said that it expects most people who have been claiming income-based jobseeker's allowance to move onto universal credit during this phase as they take up work.

April 2014: no new claims for tax credits.

The use of this date suggests that you may still be able to make a new claim for tax credits after October 2013, although this may only apply if you have already claimed tax credits earlier in the 2013/14 tax year and your claim has been broken – eg, if you stopped work but start again after October 2013. Tax credit claims can be renewed and continue during 2014/15 and 2015/16, until you are moved onto universal credit.

April 2014 to December 2015: Phase 2.

If you are still getting one of the old benefits and your circumstances have not changed, you are now transferred onto universal credit by the Department for Work and Pensions. It is unlikely that you will have been able to switch to universal credit earlier, unless you broke your claim for the benefit you were already getting. People who are covered by this phase are those in part-time work, disabled people, carers and lone parents with young children under five. The government has said that, where possible, priority will be given to people whose 'work behaviour' is most likely to benefit from universal credit – eg, if you are working fewer than 16 hours a week or have variable hours.

January 2016 to October 2017: Phase 3.

You are likely to be one of the last people to be moved onto universal credit if you are getting housing benefit but no other means-tested benefits and you are not in work. The government has said that the way those remaining will be moved will depend on local circumstances and may be done on a regional basis. It aims to work closely with local authorities to take account of their staffing resources and contractual obligations so they can plan for moving the last housing benefit claimants onto universal credit.

October 2017: transfer of benefit claims from the old system to universal credit complete.

The government intends to finalise this proposed timetable by spring 2012, but will keep it under review in order to to be able to respond to national and local changes.

6. Other planned changes to benefits

Universal credit is being designed and will be delivered at the same time as other major changes to the social security system. These are outlined in Box C.

The changes will largely be carried over into the new universal credit system. For instance, the ongoing changes to housing benefit will also apply to the way maximum housing costs are calculated in universal credit. Lone parents who are moved onto jobseeker's allowance when their youngest child reaches school age will also find that they are subject to much the same 'work-related requirements' when they are moved onto universal credit.

Similarly, between April 2011 and 2014, 1.5 million people on incapacity benefit and income support on the grounds of incapacity are being tested for entitlement to employment and support allowance. Although employment and support allowance will be abolished for most people, the test used to assess 'limited capability for work' will remain and will be used to place people into different 'conditionality groups' for universal credit.

Box C
Other changes

Some changes to current benefits and tax credits have already been introduced; others are planned in the near future.

Payment of contributory employment and support allowance will be time limited for those in the 'work-related activity group'. If you have received contributory employment and support allowance for one year, payment will stop from April 2012.

Lone parents whose youngest child is aged five (reduced from seven) will be moved from income support to jobseeker's allowance from 2012.

Social fund community care grants and crisis loans will be abolished and responsibility for replacing them will be given to local authorities and the Scottish and Welsh governments from

April 2013. Budgeting loans will be replaced by 'payments on account' of universal credit.

Disability living allowance will be abolished for working-age claimants and replaced by a personal independence payment from April 2013.

Council tax benefit will be abolished and responsibility for a replacement will be given to local authorities and the Scottish and Welsh governments from April 2013.

Total benefit payments will be capped at average earnings (with exceptions for households with someone with a disability and war widows) from April 2013.

The maximum amount of housing benefit payable to cover rent in the private sector has already been reduced. There will also be the power to reduce entitlement in the social rented sector to reflect family size from April 2013.

The rate of child benefit has already been frozen for three years from April 2011 and it is planned that child benefit will be deducted from higher rate taxpayers via the income tax system from January 2013.

Tax credits:

- the baby element has already been abolished
- the family element has been withdrawn from middle income families
- the disregard for increases in in-year income has already been reduced from £25,000 to £10,000, and will reduce further to £5,000 from April 2013
- support for childcare costs has already been cut from 80 to 70 per cent
- from April 2012, couples with children must work 24 hours a week (increased from 16) between them to qualify for working tax credit
- from April 2012, payments will not be increased during the year if a person's income decreases by less than £2,500

What CPAG says

Changes to benefits

From April 2013, disability living allowance for working-age people will be replaced by a new personal independence payment. This is expected to save over £1 billion, as the number of people entitled will be much reduced. The government has promised that no one will be worse off on universal credit and that the most severely disabled people will be supported. However, this may not apply to someone taken off disability living allowance and no longer classed as severely disabled under the new system, even though her/his condition has not changed.

Payment of contributory employment and support allowance will be limited to one year for people in the work-related activity group. This undermines the principle of paying national insurance contributions while in work in return for benefits in times of sickness.

Child benefit is a truly universal benefit (subject to immigration status) as payment does not depend on income, national insurance contributions or work-related conditions, and it recognises the value to society of bringing up children. It has proved especially valuable to women as, in most cases, it is paid directly to mothers. The value of child benefit has been eroded by a three-year freeze and its simplicity has been compromised by plans to claw it back from higher rate taxpayers from January 2013.

A 'benefit cap' will be introduced in April 2013, which will also apply to universal credit. This will mean that claimants who are out of work will get no more in benefits than the average take-home pay, projected to be £350 a week for single people and £500 for couples and lone parents. This cap could adversely affect many families with four or more children (and sometimes smaller families), depending on their housing costs.

Chapter 2
Who can claim universal credit

This chapter covers:

1. Who can claim universal credit?

2. What are the basic rules?

3. What are the financial conditions?

4. When is your entitlement restricted?

What you need to know

- To get universal credit, you must meet the basic rules of entitlement and the financial conditions.

- There are basic rules about your age, residence in Great Britain, whether you are in education and about agreeing to a 'claimant commitment', which is a kind of contract between you and the Department for Work and Pensions.

- The financial conditions are about your income and capital – eg, savings, investments and certain types of property. You cannot get universal credit if your capital is above £16,000 (although some capital is ignored). The amount of universal credit you get depends on the level of your income compared with the maximum universal credit for someone in your circumstances.

- If you are in a couple, you make a joint claim. Usually, both of you must meet the basic rules and the financial conditions.

- Even if you meet the basic rules and the financial conditions, you may have to wait a few days before your entitlement starts.

- You may not be entitled to universal credit if you meet the basic rules and financial conditions for only a short period of time.

1. Who can claim universal credit?

Universal credit is a benefit for both single people and couples on a low income to provide financial support for living costs, children, housing costs and other needs. You will be able to claim universal credit if you are in or out of work.

You will be eligible for universal credit if you meet the basic rules of entitlement and the financial conditions.

Under the current benefits system, the benefit you claim depends on your particular circumstances. For example, you can claim employment and support allowance if you are ill or disabled, or income support if you are a lone parent.

Provided you meet the basic rules and financial conditions, you will be eligible to claim universal credit regardless of your particular circumstances. For example, you will be able to claim if you are:

- a parent, including a lone parent
- ill or disabled
- a carer
- unemployed
- employed or self-employed

EXAMPLES

Who can claim universal credit

George has been made redundant. Depending on his income and his other circumstances, he can claim universal credit to provide him with some financial help.

Rosie is a lone parent working 12 hours a week in a low-paid job. One of her children is disabled, and they live in a housing association property. She can claim universal credit to provide her with some financial help.

Your specific circumstances will be taken into account to decide how much universal credit you get and to decide what you are expected to do to look for work to receive your benefit.

There is more information on the amount of universal credit you will get in Chapter 4 and on the 'work-related requirements' you may need to satisfy in Chapter 5.

Couples

If you are in a couple, you will normally make a joint claim with your partner. Both of you must satisfy the basic rules of entitlement and the financial conditions.

What the law says

Single and couple claims

- A claim can be made by a single person, or jointly by a couple. Regulations will outline some exceptions to this.

- A single person must meet the basic rules and the financial conditions for a single claim.

- A couple must each meet the basic rules and the financial conditions for a joint claim.

- There may be circumstances in which a couple is entitled to universal credit without both partners meeting the basic rules.

Sections 1, 2 and 3, and Schedule 1 paragraph 1 Welfare Reform Act 2012

You will count as a member of a couple if you are living together and you are married, or if you are living together as if you were married. If you are both of the same sex, you will count as a couple if you are living together and you are civil partners, or if you are living together as if you were civil partners. Future regulations will outline the circumstances in which you must claim as a single person even though you are a member of a couple.

There is more information about these rules in Chapter 3.

In some exceptional circumstances, it will be possible to get universal credit even though one of you does not meet the basic rules. For example, if your partner has not agreed to a 'claimant commitment' but you have, you will still be able to get universal credit. However, the amount will be reduced.

2. What are the basic rules?

There are basic rules about:

- age
- residence in Great Britain
- education
- making a 'claimant commitment'

To be entitled to universal credit, you must meet these basic rules and also meet the financial conditions.

What the law says

The basic rules

- You meet the basic rules for universal credit if you:
  - are aged 18 or over
  - are under the qualifying age for pension credit
  - are in Great Britain
  - are not in education
  - accept a claimant commitment.

- Regulations will give more details on these rules and may include exceptions.

Section 4 Welfare Reform Act 2012

Your age

You must be aged 18 or over to claim universal credit, although the government has said that exceptions will be made for younger claimants in certain circumstances. For example, lone parents or young people who are estranged from their parents may be able to claim from age 16.

You must also be below the qualifying age for pension credit. This is gradually increasing from age 60 and will reach 66 in 2020. If you are in a couple and one of you is over the qualifying age for pension credit, you will be eligible for universal credit and will not be able to choose to claim pension credit instead. The government has said that couples in this situation who are already getting pension credit will not have to move onto universal credit.

EXAMPLE

One member of a couple is over pension credit age

Charlie is 67 and his wife Joan is 58. They are eligible for universal credit. Even though Charlie is over the qualifying age for pension credit, they are not eligible for pension credit.

Joan has to meet work-related requirements as a condition of getting universal credit, but Charlie does not.

Residence in Great Britain

In general, you must be in Great Britain to claim universal credit, although there will be exceptions to this.

For example, if you are not in Great Britain, you may still be able to get universal credit if you are absent temporarily. Regulations will say how long the absence can be and in what circumstances this will be allowed. You may also be able to get universal credit if you are employed on board a ship or working on an oil rig.

In some cases, even though you are in Great Britain, you will not be able to get universal credit. This mostly applies to people coming from abroad.

- You may not be able to get universal credit if you are defined as a 'person subject to immigration control' (although there will be some exceptions).

- You may not be able to get universal credit if you are not 'habitually resident' in Great Britain. This rule applies to some current benefits and will probably apply in a similar way to universal credit.

* You may not be able to get universal credit if you do not have a 'right to reside' in Great Britain. This rule applies to many current benefits and will probably apply in a similar way to universal credit. This mostly affects nationals of countries in the European Economic Area.

Education

In general, you will not be able to claim universal credit if you are in education. However, there are likely to be exceptions to this.

The government intends 'to maintain and continue the support that is provided on an exceptional basis to people in education through the benefit system'. However, it has not yet said how this will be done.

Currently, some students in full-time education can claim existing benefits. Parents can claim tax credits for their children. Lone parents and disabled students can claim income support or employment and support allowance and housing benefit. Young students in further education can claim housing benefit to help with their rent. If they are estranged from their parents, they can also claim income support. Universal credit will replace all the current benefits that provide this support. Future regulations will set out which groups of students will be eligible for universal credit.

Making a claimant commitment

In order to be entitled to universal credit, you must make a 'claimant commitment' in which you agree to meet certain requirements. The claimant commitment will set out what you must do to receive your universal credit award and you must agree to this. The key part of a claimant commitment will be about 'work-related requirements'.

There is more information about the claimant commitment in Chapter 5.

EXAMPLE

The basic rules

Jane and Kevin are a couple, both aged 20. They are UK nationals and live in London. Neither are in education. They want to know if they can claim universal credit.

They are within the age conditions, they are in Great Britain, and they are not in education, so they can claim universal credit. They must claim jointly as a couple. They must also meet the financial conditions and agree to meet certain requirements as part of their claimant commitment.

Their income must then be compared with the maximum amount of universal credit for their circumstances to see if they get an award of universal credit and, if so, how much this will be.

3. What are the financial conditions?

To be entitled to universal credit, your savings and other capital must not be more than £16,000 and your income must not be too high.

You must also meet the basic rules.

What the law says

The financial conditions

- Your capital must be below a certain amount or, if you have a partner, your combined capital must be below a certain amount.

- Your income (or, if you have a partner, your combined income) must be sufficiently low so that you are entitled to more than a set minimum amount of universal credit.

Section 5 Welfare Reform Act 2012

What CPAG says

Who can claim

Universal credit is a single benefit with one set of rules. In deciding what these rules should be, the government has selected from the existing benefits that are being replaced. It has been suggested that, in some respects, the government has 'chosen the least favourable option that currently exists and [has] decided to apply it universally'. This concern runs through many of the conditions of entitlement for universal credit. For example:

Tax credits have no capital limit while other means-tested benefits do have a limit. Under universal credit, the capital limit will apply to everyone, penalising savers.

Jobseeker's allowance has a lower age limit of 18. This will be extended to universal credit, although there will be exceptions set out in regulations. If these exceptions are more restricted than now, some young people could be worse off under the new system. For example, a young person aged 16 or 17 living away from her/his parents who claims benefit before universal credit is introduced can get housing benefit to help with her/his rent. A young person in the same situation under universal credit may get no help with her/his rent.

Full-time students with children can currently claim child tax credit. Claiming amounts of universal credit for children may or may nor be extended to people in education. If it is not, full-time students with children will be worse off than under the current system.

In general, because there will be one benefit with one set of simplified rules, there will be situations in which someone seeking financial support after universal credit is introduced will find her/himself worse off than someone in the same circumstances claiming under the current system.

As a general principle, CPAG supports the idea of benefit simplification, but not if the approach adopted is so broad that many people on low incomes are entitled to less support.

If your capital (or, if you have a partner, your combined capital) is above the proposed limit of £16,000, you will not get any universal credit. This is similar to the current rules for most means-tested benefits (income support, jobseeker's allowance, employment and support allowance, housing benefit and council tax benefit), but is less generous than the current rules for tax credits and pension credit.

EXAMPLE

The financial conditions

Sophie is a lone parent with two children. She does not work and has savings of £20,000. Under the proposed capital rules, she does not qualify for universal credit and will not get any help to support her children.

If Sophie were to claim under the current system, she would not get any income support, housing benefit or council tax benefit, but she would get child tax credit of over £100 a week.

---

4. When is your entitlement restricted?

In some situations, you will not get universal credit even if you meet the basic rules and financial conditions.

For example, this may apply to a 'waiting period' at the start of your claim of up to seven days (in some circumstances there will be no waiting period), or if you are getting certain other benefits. It may also apply if you meet the basic rules and financial conditions for a short time only, up to a maximum of seven days.

What the law says

Restricting entitlement

- You are not entitled to universal credit if you only meet the conditions of entitlement for a short period.

- You are not entitled to universal credit for a certain length of time at the start of your claim, even if you meet the other conditions of entitlement.

- Regulations will set out other circumstances in which you are not entitled to universal credit, even if you meet the other conditions of entitlement.

Section 6 Welfare Reform Act 2012

Further information

There is more information about the current rules for means-tested benefits, on which universal credit will be based, in CPAG's *Welfare Benefits and Tax Credits Handbook*.

Chapter 3
How to claim universal credit

This chapter covers:

1. Who should claim universal credit?

2. How do you make a claim?

3. When should you claim?

4. How are you paid?

5. Reporting changes in your circumstances

6. What happens when universal credit is introduced?

What you need to know

- You must make a joint claim for universal credit if you are in a couple. If you are a lone parent or a single person, you must make a single claim.

- The usual way to claim is online, although some people can still claim by telephone or in person.

- Universal credit is normally paid directly into your bank account. Couples can have a joint account or choose which one will receive the payment.

- Payments are normally made monthly, although in exceptional circumstances they can be more frequent.

- You can check your award and payments, and report changes in your circumstances, using your online account. You may not need to report changes in your earnings as your employer will use a new 'real-time information system' to give details on your earnings every time you are paid. This is used to adjust your universal credit award.

- Universal credit is planned to be introduced in October 2013 and new claims will be accepted from then. Universal credit will be phased in for existing claimants of income support, income-based jobseeker's allowance, income-related employment and support allowance, housing benefit, child tax credit and working tax credit.

1. Who should claim universal credit?

Universal credit is a benefit to provide support for adults and children.

- If you are in a couple, you make a joint claim.
- If you are single or a lone parent, you make a single claim.

What the law says

Single and couple claims

- You make a joint claim if you are in a couple – ie, you both claim together. You make a single claim if you are not a member of a couple.

- You are in a couple if you are married or registered civil partners and living in the same household, or if you are living together as though you were married or civil partners.

- Regulations may specify certain circumstances in which you must make a claim as a single person, even though you are in a couple.

Sections 2 and 39 Welfare Reform Act 2012

Usually it is clear whether or not you are in a couple, but there are rules about this.

- You and your partner are a couple if you are married and living in the same household.

- You and your partner are a couple if you are not married but 'living together as husband and wife'.

- You and your partner are a couple if you are the same sex, and are registered as civil partners and living in the same household.

- You and your partner are a couple if you are the same sex and not civil partners, but 'living together as though you were civil partners'.

'Living together as husband and wife' and 'as though you were civil partners' are not defined. It is expected that the same factors that are used to decide if people are living together for current benefits will continue to be used in universal credit. These include the type of relationship you have, whether you have children and your financial arrangements.

Box A
Members of a couple who must claim as a single person

- You must claim as a single person if your partner is:
  - away from home and this is expected to be permanent
  - away from home and this is expected to last more than 52 weeks
  - in prison
  - abroad for longer than a set time
  - in hospital for longer than a set time
  - living in a care home.

- You must claim as a single person if other special situations apply – eg, your partner does not have a 'right to reside' in Great Britain.

The government has said these situations are likely to apply. They are based on the current income support rules. The government may make other rules to treat people as single, even if they are only temporarily apart, but does not plan to do so initially.

It will be important to claim correctly as a single person or as a couple. Claiming on the wrong basis could mean that you are overpaid and you may have to pay back universal credit. Usually it will be clear whether you are single or in a couple. However, Box A lists the circumstances in which you must make a claim as a single person, even though you have a partner.

What happens if you start or end a relationship?

You will probably not need to make a fresh claim if you were previously claiming as a single person but are now in a couple, or if you were claiming jointly as a couple but are now single or in a different couple.

However, you will have to report the change in your circumstances. Because there is likely to be no need to make a fresh claim, there should be little delay in getting your new award and continuing with your payments.

What happens if you cannot claim for yourself?

If you cannot claim for yourself, perhaps because you have a mental health problem or learning disability, someone else (called an 'appointee'), who might be a friend or relative, can be authorised to claim on your behalf. If you have a partner, s/he could make the joint claim for both of you.

2. How do you make a claim?

The government intends that claims for universal credit will be made:

- online
- by telephone if you cannot claim online
- in person if you really need to claim this way

You will need to provide all the information required for the claim, including details of your and your partner's income and savings, and the circumstances of you, your partner and dependent children. If you are working, the Department for Work and Pensions (DWP) intends to use HM Revenue and Custom's (HMRC's) proposed 'real-time information system' to gather information about your earnings. This is a new system which will require your employer to send information to HMRC every time your wages are paid. The DWP will use this information to reassess your universal credit award on a regular basis, so if your earnings are taxed through PAYE (Pay as You Earn), you will not need to report your earnings, even when they change. You will still need to report any other income you have.

What the law says

How to make a claim

- Claims are made and communication with the DWP is carried out online. The extent to which this also takes place by telephone and in writing depends on DWP policy and practice.

- Legally, decisions are made by a DWP decision maker, although in practice most assessments are automatically issued by computer.

- The transfer of existing claimants to universal credit will be phased. The DWP has flexibility in how it deals with new claims when universal credit is introduced. For example, there may be early claims and advance awards.

Sections 98 and 104, and Schedule 6 Welfare Reform Act 2012

3. When should you claim?

In general, once universal credit is introduced, if you are not already getting benefit you should claim as soon as you think you might be entitled. This might be, for example, because you have a baby or because you stop or start work. The government has not yet said whether you will be able to backdate a claim for universal credit.

If you are already getting benefit, you may be transferred to universal credit at a later date.

You might be able to claim in advance. If you make your claim at a time when you are not yet entitled to universal credit, but the Department for Work and Pensions thinks you will become entitled shortly, it can make an advance award. For example, this might help you if your income means that you are not entitled to universal credit at the start of your claim, but you will be entitled once additions (eg, to help with your mortgage interest payments) are made to your universal credit award some weeks after you claim.

EXAMPLES

When to claim

In November 2013, Amina has her first baby. She is aged 20 and is a lone parent. She rents her home. She has never claimed benefit before. She claims universal credit to support herself and her baby, and to help with her rent. She completes the form and makes her claim online.

In December 2013, John is made redundant. His partner, Alex, is working part time and they have a child. John and Alex claim universal credit to top up Alex's part-time wages. They make the claim online, jointly.

Getting your decision

The responsibility for making a decision on your claim will lie with a decision maker in the Department for Work and Pensions. In practice, in most cases, the assessment of your claim and the calculation of your award will be done automatically by computer.

Your award will be assessed over a set period. The government intends that awards will be assessed (and paid) monthly.

4. How are you paid?

Universal credit will be paid directly into your bank account or building society account in monthly payments.

If you find it difficult to budget with monthly payments, it may be possible to be paid more frequently. There will be a 'payment exceptions service' for this. However, this will be discretionary and you will need to show that you are in exceptional circumstances.

What the law says

Payments

- Regulations will say when a couple can decide which of them will be paid universal credit. Regulations will allow the Department for Work and Pensions (DWP) to decide that the other partner should be paid instead.

- Regulations will say when payments can be made if there is a delay in deciding a universal credit claim. This is called 'payment on account'.

- Regulations will also say when a payment on account can be made in cases of need or in other specified situations.

- Regulations will allow direct payments to be made from universal credit to third parties, such as mortgage lenders.

Sections 100 and 101, and Schedule 2, paragraphs 5 and 6 Welfare Reform Act 2012

If you are in a couple and claiming jointly, the government intends that universal credit will normally be paid in a single payment to the household. It will be up to you to decide which of you will get this. If you cannot decide, the DWP can make the decision. Regulations will permit universal credit to be split between partners. However, the government has said that making split payments will be exceptional – eg, if there is hardship or in the case of a relationship breakdown.

EXAMPLE

Payments to couples

Anna and Viktor claim universal credit jointly as a couple. They have two children. Viktor is working full time and all the universal credit is paid into his bank account. He gives Anna money regularly but it does not cover food, bills and rent, all of which she is expected to pay. Viktor will not agree to the benefit being paid directly to Anna instead. Anna can ask the DWP either to pay her instead of Viktor, or to split the payment between them.

What can you do if there is a delay in getting paid?

If there is a delay in deciding your universal credit claim, you will be able to get an advance payment. This is known as a 'payment on account'. If there is a delay on only one part of your claim (eg, if there is still some information or evidence needed to decide how much housing costs to pay), the government has said that you will be able to get the remainder of your universal credit award in the meantime as a payment on account.

Under the current benefits system, you can claim a crisis loan if your benefit claim is delayed. Under universal credit, there will be no crisis loans and you must ask for a payment on account instead.

EXAMPLE

Payment on account because of a delay

Carmine is a lone parent with one child. She works part time and rents her home. Carmine claims universal credit. She has been asked to provide proof of the rent she pays, but she does not have a rent book and is having trouble getting the evidence she needs from her landlord. Rather than holding up all her claim, the Department for Work and Pensions decides in the meantime to pay Carmen all her universal credit, except for her housing costs, as a payment on account.

What can you do if you need a loan?

If you need a loan for something you cannot afford, you will be able to ask for an advance of universal credit (called a 'payment on account'). This will replace the current social fund budgeting loans. Regulations will set out the qualifying conditions, the maximum amount you can get and the repayment terms. The Department for Work and Pensions (DWP) plans that advances will be available to people who have been on universal credit for 26 weeks. It is expected that there will be detailed guidance to decision makers on how to decide whether someone should get a payment on account.

In order to get this kind of payment, you must be able to pay it back. Repayment will normally be made from your ongoing universal credit, but the DWP will have other ways of recovering the payment – eg, from your earnings or by taking action through the courts.

EXAMPLE

Payment on account as a loan

Emma is a lone parent and is getting universal credit. Her washing machine has broken down and she needs a new one. Instead of buying one with expensive high street credit, she asks for a payment on account of her universal credit. She pays this back at a set rate out of her benefit.

Paying universal credit to other people

Regulations will allow the Department for Work and Pensions (DWP) to pay part of your universal credit directly to a third party on your behalf. For example, if you have a mortgage, the amount in your universal credit for mortgage interest may be paid directly to your lender.

If you rent your home, the government has said that it plans to pay the amount for rent in your universal credit to you and not to your landlord, irrespective of whether you rent from a local authority, housing association or private landlord. However, it is expected that there will still be a facility for direct payments to landlords in some circumstances.

Claims and payments

CPAG is concerned about the potential effects of a number of the proposals, including the frequency of payments, that payments are made to just one person in the household, and that a single payment could be 'all or nothing'.

With payments expected to be monthly instead of fortnightly as they are at present, there is concern that many people on low incomes will find it hard to budget. When this happens, mothers in particular tend to go without.

With support for adults and children included in one payment, there should be a guarantee that money meant for children should go to the main carer, usually the mother.

In the current benefits system, it is common for a claim to be delayed or for payments to be suspended while the DWP clarifies evidence or waits to make a decision. Under universal credit, all support depends on one payment and so the consequences of delay or suspension could be that someone is left with no means of support.

If, as well as monthly payments, there are to be monthly reassessments of all income and circumstances and not just of earnings under the new real-time information system, a monthly reporting requirement is likely to prove difficult for many, and impossible for some, claimants. For those who are self-employed and not part of the real-time information system, a monthly update will be complex and bureaucratic, and likely to act as a barrier to people entering self-employment.

CPAG is concerned that people will lose out when social fund budgeting loans and crisis loans are abolished in favour of payments on account. The social fund provides crucial support to low-income families. The new system could mean that less money is available to people in need, and more people could resort to high-cost doorstep lenders.

5. Reporting changes in your circumstances

You will have an online account for your universal credit award. This will allow you to check the information about your claim and payments, and also will mean you can report changes in your circumstances online. If you cannot use the internet, there will be other ways to report changes in your circumstances – eg, by telephone or face-to-face with an adviser.

The government intends that if you are employed, you will not need to report changes in your earnings. The Department for Work and Pensions will obtain information on your earnings from HM Revenue and Customs (HMRC) through its new 'real-time information system'. Under this system, your employer sends HMRC information about your earnings every time you are paid.

You will have to report other changes in your circumstances that might affect your entitlement to universal credit or how much you get. There might be certain changes that you are required to report, even though they do not affect your entitlement – eg, changes that might affect which 'conditionality group' you are in.

There is more information on conditionality groups in Chapter 5.

Note: you should report any changes in your circumstances promptly. If you do not, you might be overpaid or underpaid. You may also be fined (called a 'civil penalty').

There is more information on fines in Chapter 6.

6. What happens when universal credit is introduced?

If you are already getting one of the benefits that are to be abolished when universal credit is introduced (income support, income-based jobseeker's allowance, income-related employment and support allowance, housing benefit, child tax credit and working tax credit), you will stay on that benefit until either your circumstances change or the Department for Work and Pensions (DWP) decides it is time to transfer your claim to universal credit. You will not be able to choose to claim universal credit instead of the benefit you are already getting. The transfer process for all existing claimants is due to begin in April 2014 and end by 2017.

There is more information about the transfer in Chapter 1.

If you are nearing pension age, you might not be transferred to universal credit at all. The details of this will be in regulations that are still to be published.

The government has not yet decided in what order existing claimants will transfer onto universal credit. However, when you *do* transfer to the new system, you will not need to make a separate claim. The transfer will be automatic.

If you are entitled to universal credit, 'transitional protection' will make sure that the amount you get when you move onto universal credit will be the same as you were getting on your previous benefit.

Bearing in mind that the rules for universal credit will not be the same as the rules for current benefits, you may find that you do not qualify for universal credit, despite having been entitled to an existing benefit. You may be allowed to get universal credit in this situation even though you do not qualify. Regulations will set out how this will work.

The DWP will have a lot of flexibility in how it deals with claims shortly before and after universal credit is introduced. For example, if you try to claim universal credit before you are allowed to do so (eg, because you are in a group that is due to be transferred later), your claim can be treated as a claim for an existing benefit.

Chapter 4
The amount of universal credit

This chapter covers:

1. The maximum amount of universal credit

2. How does your income and capital affect universal credit?

3. How much universal credit will you get?

What you need to know

- Universal credit includes amounts for you and your partner. This is called the 'standard allowance'.

- Amounts for any children for whom you are responsible are added to the standard allowance.

- Extra amounts are also added to the standard allowance, depending on your circumstances. There is an additional amount if someone in your family is ill or disabled, provided s/he meets the qualifying conditions. There is also an additional amount if you or your partner are caring for a disabled person. There are also amounts for rent and mortgage costs, and for childcare costs.

- If you have other income, this reduces the amount of universal credit to which you are entitled, although some income is ignored.

- You are not entitled to universal credit if you have more than £16,000 in capital.

1. The maximum amount of universal credit

Universal credit is a 'means-tested' benefit. This means that the amount you get depends on your family circumstances and on how much other income (if any) you have. As your income increases, the amount of your universal credit award will reduce.

Your maximum universal credit will be made up of the total of:

- a 'standard allowance'
- an amount for each child
- an amount for each disabled child (at a lower or higher rate)
- an amount for an ill or disabled adult (at a lower or higher rate)
- an amount for a carer
- an amount for housing costs
- an amount for childcare costs

Each of the above amounts has its own qualifying conditions. The rest of this section explains when these amounts apply and how your maximum amount of universal credit will be worked out. There are examples at the end of the section.

Amount for you and your family

Universal credit will include an amount for you, your partner and any children you have.

What the law says

Amounts for you and your family

- The amount for you and your partner is called the 'standard allowance'.

- Added to the standard allowance is an amount for any children for whom you are responsible.

- Regulations may allow an additional amount to be included in your universal credit if your child has a disability.

Sections 9 and 10 Welfare Reform Act 2012

The amount in universal credit for you and your partner (if you have one) is called the 'standard allowance'. How much you get depends on whether you are making a single claim or a joint claim. The government intends to set the standard allowance at the same level as the existing jobseeker's allowance rates. In 2012/13 these were:

- £71 a week for a single person
- £111.45 a week for a couple

If you are under 25, your standard allowance may be less – £56.25 a week for a single person at the current rates.

These amounts will be uprated by the time universal credit is introduced in 2013.

There may be situations when you will not get a standard allowance, even though you continue to be entitled to universal credit – eg, if you are in prison for a short period of time.

If you are responsible for a child or children, your universal credit will include additional amounts (called the 'child responsibility element') for each child under 16 and for each young person who is 16 or over and, for example, is still at school or college on a non-advanced course. There are likely to be situations in which you will not be treated as responsible for a child, even though s/he lives with you – eg, if you are caring for a child who is 'looked after' by local authority. Future regulations will set out exactly when an award will include amounts for a child or young person.

Only one claimant (a single person or a couple) will be able to claim for a particular child. The amount for a child is planned to be at the same level as child tax credit. In 2012/13, this was around £51.59 a week.

Child tax credit includes a family element (one per household) of £10.50 a week. If universal credit is to maintain the current basic rates of support for children, this amount will have to be included. One option for doing so would be to add it to the universal credit amount for a claimant's first child. This would mean that the additional amount for a first child would be £62.09 and £51.59 for any other children.

Additional amount if your child is disabled

If your child is disabled, your universal credit will include an extra amount. The government intends there to be two different levels of payment depending on the severity of your child's disability. Entitlement to these extra amounts will depend on your child getting disability living allowance (or getting personal independence payment at the appropriate rate if s/he is 16 or over) or having a severe visual impairment.

- The lower amount is planned to be around £28.15 a week (at 2012/13 rates).

- The higher amount, which will depend on the child getting the highest rate care component of disability living allowance or having a severe visual impairment (ie, s/he must be registered or certified as blind), will be around £77 a week.

What CPAG says

Amounts for disabled children

At 2012/13 rates, the disability element in child tax credit is £56.63 a week. For the most severely disabled children, this rises to £79.45 a week.

CPAG is concerned that many families with a disabled child will lose out under universal credit. It is estimated that the parents of around 100,000 disabled children will receive only half the amount of the disability addition they get under the current system (although initially people already getting benefit will continue to get the same amount). This could mean a total loss of £22,000 for each family by the time a child reaches 16.

Additional amount if you or your partner are ill or disabled

If you or your partner are ill or disabled, you may get an additional amount added to your 'standard allowance'.

What the law says

Addition for an ill or disabled adult

An additional amount may be added to the standard allowance if you have limited capability for work or limited capability for work-related activity.

Section 12 Welfare Reform Act 2012

Box A
Limited capability for work test

'Limited capability for work' is a test of whether your health problems or disabilities mean that you are currently unable to work. It is also used to decide whether you qualify for employment and support allowance. The assessment normally involves your filling in a questionnaire and attending a medical examination. In some circumstances, you are treated as having limited capability for work without having to go through this assessment. For example, this applies if you:

- are a hospital inpatient or recovering from treatment in hospital
- are in residential rehabilitation for drug or alcohol problems
- are pregnant and your baby is either due within six weeks, or there would be a serious risk to your health or the health of your baby if you were expected to work or look for work
- gave birth less than two weeks ago (this may be longer if you get maternity allowance)

You may be assessed regularly to check whether you still meet these conditions. If you do not return the questionnaire about your health problems or do not attend the medical without good reason, you are treated as not satisfying the conditions. If you receive employment and support allowance, you will probably not need to have a separate assessment for universal credit.

Box B
Limited capability for work-related activity test

The severity of your health problems is decided by looking at whether or not you have a 'limited capability for work-related activity'. This test is designed to identify whether your illness or disability is so serious that, currently, you should not be expected to think about returning to work. You are treated as having limited capability for work-related activity without having to go through the assessment if:

• you are terminally ill
• you receive certain types of chemotherapy, have done so in the last six months or are likely to do so in the next six months
• you are pregnant and there would be a serious risk to your health or the health of your baby if you did any work-related activity
• there would be a serious risk to your physical or mental health or to that of anyone else if it is decided that you do not have a limited capability for work-related activity

You may be regularly assessed to check whether you still meet these conditions. If you receive employment and support allowance, you will probably not need to have a separate assessment for universal credit.

The government intends there to be two different levels of this addition, reflecting the severity of your difficulties.

• There will be a lower amount, probably around £28.15 a week (at 2012/13 rates), if you are assessed as having 'limited capability for work' (see Box A).

• There will be a higher amount if you are more severely disabled and are assessed as having 'limited capability for work-related activity' (see Box B). This is likely to be around £34.05 a week, although the government intends this to rise to around £77 a week, as 'resources become available'.

If both partners in a couple have limited capability for work, there is no indication that they will get two additions. If universal credit follows the current employment and support allowance rules, this will not be the case.

You will not be able to get this addition and a carer's addition (see below) at the same time. If you are in a couple, however, one of you could get this addition while the other could get the carer's addition, provided you both qualify.

EXAMPLE

Addition for a disabled adult

Seb is aged 25 and is severely disabled. He receives the higher rate mobility component and the highest rate care component of disability living allowance. He lives alone and no one receives carer's allowance for him.

Under income support, his entitlement (excluding housing costs) would be:

Personal allowance £71.00

Disability premium £30.35

Enhanced disability premium £14.80

Severe disability premium £58.20

Total = £174.35

Under universal credit, his entitlement (excluding housing costs) is:

Standard allowance £71.00

Amount for limited capability for work-related activity £77.00*

Total = £148.00

Net weekly loss = £26.35

*Note: this is the amount the government hopes to pay, as 'resources become available'. When universal credit is first introduced, it is likely to be significantly lower.

When you claim universal credit, it is likely that there will be a 'waiting period' before you get this additional amount. This is likely to reflect the current system for employment and support allowance, in which most claimants have to wait 13 weeks before receiving any additional component.

What CPAG says

Amounts for ill or disabled adults

The government has said that the current system of disability premiums and additions is 'difficult to deliver, can be prone to error and confusing for disabled people'. The proposed structure and rates of the additional amounts in universal credit may be more straightforward, but will be far less generous for many people. It is likely to result in a significant loss in income for many disabled people.

Additional amount if you or your partner are a carer

If you are caring for someone who is severely disabled, you will get an additional amount in your universal credit.

What the law says

Addition for a carer

An additional amount may be added to the standard allowance for particular needs or circumstances – eg, if you are caring for a severely disabled person.

Section 12 Welfare Reform Act 2012

You will be able to get an additional amount (a 'carer element') if you are caring for a severely disabled person for at least 35 hours a week. This is likely to mean that the person being cared for is getting attendance allowance, the care component of disability living allowance paid at either the middle or highest rate, or the daily living component of the proposed new personal independence payment.

The government has not yet said how much the carer element will be. You will not be able to get this addition and the addition for either 'limited capability for work' or 'limited capability for work-related activity' at the same time. However, if you are in a couple and you qualify, one of you could get the carer's addition and the other partner could get the limited capability for work/limited capability for work-related activity addition.

Amount for housing costs

Universal credit will include an amount for certain housing costs.

What the law says

Housing costs

- Universal credit includes an amount for the housing costs of the home in which you normally live.

- Your home must be in Great Britain.

- Regulations will say which housing costs count and when they do not count.

- There may be circumstances in which your housing costs are not included from the start of your claim – ie, there may be a 'waiting period'.

- There may be circumstances in which your housing costs are only paid for a limited period of time.

Section 11 Welfare Reform Act 2012

Housing costs can be either rent or mortgage interest payments and may also include certain service charges.

The amount you will get to help you with your rent will depend on how many people are in your family and on your circumstances. If you are living in the social rented sector (ie, you are renting from a local authority or housing association), the amount may be limited if you are considered to be living in a property that is too big for you.

If you are living in the private rented sector, the amount is likely to be limited to reflect the lowest one-third of market rents available. Other limitations, such as the size of property you need, will also be applied. There will be an overall ceiling on the amount of rent that universal credit will cover for a particular size of property.

The amount you will get to help with your mortgage interest payments is likely to have an upper limit. It will probably be calculated using a standard interest rate, which will not necessarily cover the actual amount of mortgage interest that you must pay.

The government will be able to limit the circumstances in which you can get help with your housing costs. For example, you may not get help as soon as you start claiming universal credit and the help you get may only be paid for a limited period of time (probably two years). It is likely that this will only apply to you if you have mortgage interest to pay. It is not expected that the time limit will be applied to people renting their home. It is also likely that you will not get help with your mortgage interest if you are in paid work.

Amount for childcare costs

The government has said that, if you are working, universal credit will include help with 'formal' childcare costs – eg, a registered childminder, nursery or after-school club. This will apply even if you are working for less than 16 hours a week. If you are a lone parent, you will be able to get help with childcare costs irrespective of how many hours you work and, if you are a couple, you will be eligible if both of you are working.

EXAMPLE

Childcare costs

Amara is a lone parent with one child. She has childcare costs of £150 a week. Under the proposed system, Amara will get £105 a week in her maximum universal credit amount for childcare costs – ie, 70 per cent of £150.

What CPAG says

Childcare costs

CPAG is concerned that the proposed provision for childcare costs will make work much less affordable for many parents. Current rules allowing childcare costs to be disregarded for housing benefit and council tax benefit mean that, in practice, many parents are able to recoup up to 95.5 per cent of their childcare costs. A reduction to 70 per cent therefore represents a significant increase in their childcare outgoings. This development takes place at a time when the cost of childcare is rising significantly. Instead of more parents entering work, we may see more parents leaving work because the childcare that enables them to work is no longer sufficiently affordable to make them better off.

It is likely that a percentage of your childcare costs (probably 70 per cent) will be included in your maximum universal credit, up to a maximum amount. The government has indicated that the maximum amounts will be £175 a week for one child and £300 a week for two or more children, so the most you will be able to get is £122 a week for one child or £210 for two or more children – ie, 75 per cent of £175 or £300.

EXAMPLES

Maximum universal credit

Mike and Sharmani are a couple with two children. Neither has health problems. The couple have a mortgage of £50,000. They have no childcare costs.

Maximum universal credit:

Standard allowance £111.45

Amount for children £113.68

Amount for housing costs £34.90

Total = £260.03

Note: the above figures are based on what the government has said the rates are likely to be. The housing costs are based on a standard interest rate of 3.63 per cent, which is the rate currently used to calculate housing costs for income support.

Marcia is a lone parent with one child. She lives in a housing association house and her rent is £110 a week. The house is the right size for her and her child. The child has a disability and gets the lowest rate care component of disability living allowance. She has childcare costs of £50 a week.

Maximum universal credit:
Standard allowance £71.00

Amount for child £62.09

Amount for disabled child £28.15

Amount for housing costs £110.00

Amount for childcare £35.00

Total = £306.24

Note: the above figures are based on what the government has said the rates are likely to be. The housing costs are based on Marcia getting the full amount of rent for a house in the social rented sector which she is not under-occupying. The childcare costs are based on the proposal that 70 per cent of actual costs, up to a maximum of £125 for one child, will be included in the maximum universal credit calculation.

2. How does your income and capital affect universal credit?

If you and your partner have any income or capital, your universal credit may be affected. Your income could be your earnings or other income, such as other benefits. Your capital includes savings and some property. As your income increases, the amount of universal credit you get will usually decrease. Income belonging to your children is ignored.

> ### What the law says
>
> #### Income
>
> - Earned income and unearned income is deducted from the maximum amount of universal credit.
>
> - Some income is disregarded.
>
> - Regulations will set out the rate of the deduction.
>
> - Income means your own income if you are a single claimant or your combined income if you are a couple claiming jointly.
>
> *Section 8(3) and (4) Welfare Reform Act 2012*

Earnings

Your net earnings (after tax, national insurance and half of any contribution to an occupational pension scheme) may affect your universal credit. If you are self-employed and on a low income, you may be assumed to have a higher level of earnings – eg, the equivalent of full-time earnings on the national minimum wage.

Statutory sick pay and statutory maternity, paternity and adoption pay will count as earnings. This means that this type of income will be subject to the 'earnings disregard' (see below) and 'taper' (see page 53).

You will be able to keep a certain amount of your earnings before your universal credit is affected. This is called the 'earnings disregard'. The government has said that the maximum weekly earnings disregard levels are likely to be approximately as set out in the table on page 53.

If your universal credit includes housing costs, the earnings disregard will be reduced. The government intends that your disregard will be reduced by one and a half times the amount of housing costs you receive in your universal credit. However, the disregard will only be reduced to a minimum 'disregard floor'. This amount will depend on your circumstances. You will get the highest disregard that applies to you. The government has not yet decided who will come into the disabled worker category.

Note: a household can only receive one disregard.

Disregarded earnings		
Circumstances	Minimum weekly disregard	Maximum weekly disregard
Single person (no children)	£13.46	£13.46
Couple (no children)	£36.92	£57.69
Couple (with children)	£36.92, plus £10 for first child and £5 each for second and third child	£139.42
Lone parent	£43.46, plus £10 for first child and £5 each for second and third child	£173.08
Disabled person	£40	£134.62

How do your earnings affect universal credit?

Once you have worked out which disregard applies to you and how much of your earnings count, the maximum universal credit is reduced by a proportion of this figure. This is often called the 'taper' – ie, the rate at which your universal credit will 'taper' away as your earnings increase. It is likely that the taper for universal credit will be 65 per cent. This means that as your earnings increase above the level that is disregarded, your universal credit will decrease by 65 pence for every extra pound you earn.

There are examples of how this works on pages 59 and 60.

Other income

Any other income you have may affect your universal credit. Some income such as disability living allowance, personal independence payment, child benefit and child maintenance will be disregarded. It

EXAMPLES

Couple with two children

Jon and Barry's maximum weekly earnings disregard is £139.42.

They have housing costs in their universal credit of £80 a week.

£80 x 1.5 = £120.

Their earnings disregard of £139.42 is reduced by this amount, but only to a minimum (the disregard floor) of £51.92.

This means that their actual earnings disregard is £51.92 a week.

Disabled person

Uche's maximum weekly earnings disregard is £134.62.

She has housing costs in her universal credit of £60 a week.

£60 x 1.5 = £90.

Her earnings disregard of £134.62 is reduced by this amount.

This means that her actual earnings disregard is £44.62. The disregard floor does not impact on her, as her disregard is still above the appropriate minimum amount for a person in her situation (£40).

Lone parent with three children

Ildiko's maximum weekly earnings disregard is £173.08.

She has no housing costs in her universal credit. This means that her earnings disregard remains at £173.08.

is likely that other benefits, such as carer's allowance, will be taken into account in full. Occupational pensions and spousal maintenance will also count in full. Other income (apart from earnings) will reduce your maximum universal credit pound for pound, unless it is disregarded.

Income from capital

Any capital you have may affect your universal credit. 'Capital' includes savings, stocks and shares, property and trusts. Certain types of capital will be ignored – eg, property which is your main home, personal injury payments placed in a trust fund, some other compensation payments and business assets. It is likely that there will be regulations exempting the proceeds from the sale of a former home from being included as capital – eg, if they are earmarked to buy a new home. This kind of exemption will probably be time-limited to 26 weeks. Any capital owned by your children is ignored.

If you and your partner have capital of over £16,000, you will not be able to get universal credit. If your capital is over £6,000 but £16,000 or less, you will be treated as having an income of £1 a week for every £250 (or part of £250) over £6,000. For example, if you have £7,400 capital, you will be treated as having an income from this capital of £6 a week.

3. How much universal credit will you get?

Calculate universal credit

What the law says

How universal is calculated

A universal credit award is worked out in the following way.

Step 1: Add together the maximum amount for you and your family.

Step 2: Work out your earnings and how much can be ignored.

Step 3: Work out any other income you have and how much can be ignored.

Step 4: Work out your total income.

Step 5: Calculate the amount of universal credit to which you are entitled.

Section 8 Welfare Reform Act 2012

To work out how much universal credit you will get, you must start by calculating the maximum amount payable for a person in your situation. If you have any other income, it may affect how much you get. Earned income is treated differently from unearned income, such as other benefits. Follow the steps below to work out your entitlement. We have used weekly figures throughout this section to make it easier to compare with the benefits and tax credits being replaced by universal credit, although it is likely that universal credit will be paid monthly.

Note: it is likely that there will be an overall 'benefit cap' on the amount of universal credit. There is more information on this on page 62.

Step 1: calculate your maximum universal credit

Add together the 'standard allowance', any additional amounts because you have children, any additional amounts for special circumstances (such as ill health, caring responsibilities and childcare costs) and any housing costs. The total is your maximum universal credit.

If you have no other income, this is the amount of universal credit you will get.

If you have other income, go to Step 2.

Step 2: work out your income other than earnings

Your income might comprise other benefits (such as contributory employment and support allowance), an occupational pension or an 'assumed' income from any capital you have over the lower limit. Remember that some benefits, including disability living allowance and child benefit, are ignored.

If you have no unearned income, go to Step 4.

Step 3: deduct the answer at Step 2 from the answer at Step 1

If you have no earned income, this is the amount of universal credit you will get.

If you have earned income, go to Step 4.

Step 4: work out your earnings
Work out your net earnings, after tax, national insurance and half of any contribution you make to an occupational pension.

Step 5: work out how much of your earnings count
Check which 'earnings disregard' applies to you. If you have housing costs, reduce this disregard by one and a half times the amount of housing costs in your maximum universal credit to the 'disregard floor' that applies to you. Deduct the disregard from your net earnings (Step 4).

Calculate 65 per cent of this figure.

Step 6: work out how your earnings affect your universal credit
Deduct the answer at Step 5 from Step 1 if you have no unearned income, or from Step 3 if you have unearned income as well as earnings.

This is the amount of universal credit you will get.

Note: in the following examples, the figures used are based on what the government has said the rates are likely to be.

EXAMPLE

Lone parent with two children

Sophia lives in housing association rented property which is the right size for the family. Her rent is £120 a week. She does not have any health problems and she is not looking after a severely disabled person. Her children do not have any disabilities. She has no other income apart from child benefit. Her weekly universal credit is calculated as follows.

Step 1: maximum universal credit
Standard allowance £71.00

Amount for two children £113.68

Amount for housing costs £120.00

Total: £304.68

Sofia has no income apart from child benefit, which is likely to be disregarded for universal credit. She therefore gets the maximum amount of universal credit (£304.68). She does not need to follow the remaining steps.

EXAMPLE

Couple with one child

Bob and Gwen live in a flat and have a mortgage of £60,000. Their child has a disability and receives the lowest rate care component of disability living allowance. Their only other income is child benefit and contributory employment and support allowance of £99.15, which Bob gets because he has limited capability for work. Their weekly universal credit is calculated as follows.

Step 1: calculate maximum universal credit
Standard allowance £111.45

Amount for one child £62.09

Amount for disabled child £28.15

Amount for limited capability for work £28.15

Amount for housing costs £41.88

Total = £271.72

Step 2: work out your income other than earnings
Employment and support allowance £99.15

Step 3: deduct the answer at Step 2 from the answer at Step 1
Maximum universal credit £271.72 *minus*

Employment and support allowance £99.15

= £172.57

Because they do not have any earned income, this is the amount of universal credit they will get. They do not need to follow the remaining steps.

Note: disability living allowance and child benefit are disregarded, but employment and support allowance is deducted. The amount for housing costs is based on a standard interest rate of 3.63 per cent, which is the rate currently used to calculate housing costs for income support.

EXAMPLE

Single person

Imran is single and has no children. He has a disability and receives the middle rate care component and higher rate mobility component of disability living allowance. It is accepted that he has limited capability for work. He lives in a housing association flat which is the right size for him. His rent is £100 a week. Imran also has net earnings of £96 a week. His universal credit is calculated as follows.

Step 1: calculate maximum universal credit
Standard allowance £71.00

Amount for limited capability for work £28.15

Amount for housing costs £100.00

Total = £199.15

Step 2: work out income other than earnings
Disability living allowance is disregarded and therefore Imran has no income apart from his earnings. He can go to Step 4.

Step 4: work out your earnings
Imran has £96 a week net earnings.

Step 5: work out how much of your earnings count
The earnings disregard which applies to Imran is £134.62 less one and a half times his housing costs, which equals £150.

£134.62 – £150 = –£15.38.

This is less than the minimum disregard of £40 which applies to Imran, so therefore the disregard of £40 applies.

£56 a week of Imran's earnings counts as income (£96 – £40).

£56 x 65% = £36.40

Step 6: work out how your earnings affect your universal credit
Deduct the answer at Step 5 from the answer at Step 1 because Imran has no unearned income.

£199.15 – £36.40 = **£162.75**.

This is Imran's universal credit award.

EXAMPLE

Couple with one child

Carl and Meg are a couple with one child. Meg works and earns £150 net a week. Carl is on contributory employment and support allowance of £99.15 a week because he has limited capability for work. Their only other income is child benefit. They live in a housing association house which is the right size for them. The rent is £110 a week. They have no childcare costs. Their universal credit is calculated as follows.

Step 1: calculate maximum universal credit
Standard allowance £111.45

Amount for one child £62.09

Amount for limited capability for work £28.15

Amount for housing costs £110.00

Total £311.69

Step 2: work out income other than earnings

Carl's employment and support allowance of £99.15 counts in full as income.

Step 3: deduct the answer at Step 2 from the answer at Step 1

£311.69 – £99.15 = £212.54

Step 4: work out your earnings

Meg has £150 a week earnings.

Step 5: work out how much of your earnings count

The earnings disregard which applies to Meg and Carl is £139.42 less one and a half times their housing costs, which equals £165.

£139.42 – £165 = –£25.58

This is less than the minimum disregard of £46.92 which applies to Meg and Carl, so therefore the disregard of £46.92 applies.

£103.08 a week of Meg's earnings counts as income (£150 – £46.92).

£103.08 x 65% = £67.

Step 6 : work out how your earnings affect your universal credit

Deduct the answer at Step 5 from the answer at Step 3 as they have unearned income as well as earnings.

£212.54 – £67 = £145.54

This is Carl and Meg's universal credit award.

Are you being transferred to universal credit from another benefit?

If you are already getting one of the benefits that will be abolished when universal credit is introduced (income support, income-based jobseeker's allowance, income-related employment and support allowance, housing benefit, child tax credit and working tax credit), you will stay on that benefit until the Department for Work and

Pensions decides it is time to transfer your claim to universal credit. This transfer process is due to begin in April 2014 and end by 2017.

What the law says

Transferring to universal credit

If you are transferred to universal credit from one or more of the benefits that are being abolished, the amount of universal credit you get at the point of transfer will be no less than the amount you were previously receiving.

Schedule 6 paragraph 4(3) Welfare Reform Act 2012

If you then become entitled to universal credit, 'transitional protection' will ensure that the amount you get when you move onto universal credit will be the same as you were getting on your previous benefit. The government has said that no one will lose out as a result of the transfer to universal credit if their circumstances remain the same. You will stay on the same level of benefit, without any increases (if your circumstances do not change), until the universal credit amounts catch up over time. You will only get this transitional protection if your claim is transferred for you, not if you are allowed to claim universal credit because of a change in circumstances. Regulations will outline the kind of changes in circumstances that will result in your losing your transitional protection.

The benefit cap

The 'benefit cap' will mean that your benefit entitlement will be capped at the level of average household earnings. This will include universal credit and most other benefits, but will not include pension credit, retirement pension or childcare costs that are included in universal credit.

What the law says

The benefit cap

- Regulations will set a maximum level at which your universal credit and 'other welfare benefits' will be capped.

- 'Other welfare benefits' do not include pension credit or retirement pension.

- The maximum level will be set according to 'estimated average earnings' – ie, the average weekly earnings of a working household in Great Britain, after deductions for tax and national insurance.

- Some people are exempt from the benefit cap.

Sections 96 and 97 Welfare Reform Act 2012

Are you exempt from the benefit cap?

Some people will be exempt from having their benefits capped. These include people getting disability living allowance or personal independence payment and war widows or war widowers. There will also be an exemption for 'working families on universal credit', although the government has not explained exactly who this will be.

Being a carer in itself does not mean you are exempt from the benefit cap, although you will be exempt if you or your partner are getting disability living allowance or personal independence payment.

How much is the benefit cap?

The government intends the cap on benefits to be the same as average earnings, estimated at:

- £350 a week for a single person
- £500 for a couple or lone parent

What CPAG says

The benefit cap

According to the government, the benefit cap is based on fairness because it will prevent households on benefits having a higher income than those in work. The comparison is not, however, made on a like-for-like basis, as it does not take into account the full income of in-work households in comparable situations. This is because only wages are counted and not in-work benefits, whereas these benefits are included for out-of-work claimants who could be hit by the cap.

The government estimates that around 50,000 households will lose an average of £93 a week as a result of the cap. More than 90 per cent of those affected are likely to be families with children; 80 per cent will be families with three or more children; 40 per cent will be families with five or more children.

Other factors that seem not to have been considered by the government include the impact on kinship carers, merged families, households placed by local authorities in temporary accommodation and couples, who will be given a strong economic incentive to separate.

CPAG believes that the cap is unfair and damaging to children, and should be removed. At the very least, benefits for children, such as child benefit and amounts for children in universal credit, should be removed from the cap.

Further information

There is more information about the 'limited capability for work test' and the 'limited capability for work-related activity test' in CPAG's *Welfare Benefits and Tax Credits Handbook*.

Chapter 5
Looking for work

This chapter covers:

1. What is the claimant commitment?

2. What are you expected to do?

3. Who has no work-related requirements?

4. Who must take part in work-focused interviews?

5. Who must prepare for work?

6. Who must look for work?

What you need to know

- When you claim universal credit, you (and your partner if you have one) must accept a 'claimant commitment'. This is a kind of contract between you and the Department for Work and Pensions.

- Your claimant commitment lists your 'work-related requirements' while getting universal credit. You are placed in one of four groups, depending on your circumstances. These vary from not having to do anything, to looking for work in the same way as you must do for jobseeker's allowance.

- Undertaking certain activity to get benefit is called 'conditionality'. The intention of conditionality is to encourage you to work and not claim benefits. However, the government accepts that some groups will need to claim universal credit in the longer term. If you are in one of these groups, you may have no work-related requirements at all.

- You (and your partner if you have one) must meet a set of personalised conditions.

- Some people who already work are expected to look for more work or better paid work if their earnings are low.

1. What is the claimant commitment?

If you claim universal credit, you will normally have to agree a 'claimant commitment' before you can get any benefit.

What the law says

The claimant commitment

- You (and your partner if you have one) must usually agree a claimant commitment to be entitled to universal credit.

- The claimant commitment records your responsibilities in terms of your universal credit award. It must include a statement of the conditionality group that you are in.

- The content of the claimant commitment is set by the Department for Work and Pensions, which also decides when to change it. You must have agreed the most recent version of your claimant commitment.

Sections 4(1)(e) and 14 Welfare Reform Act 2012

What does a claimant commitment include?

The idea of the 'claimant commitment' is a new one. It will replace the 'jobseeker's agreement' used for jobseeker's allowance, but some of the content is likely to be similar. The claimant commitment will also apply to employment and support allowance, and to income support until it is abolished.

Your claimant commitment will say what you must do to be entitled to benefit. If you must look for work, it will include the number of hours you are expected to be available for work. This may be fewer than full-time hours if you are allowed to restrict your availability for work – eg, if you are the 'responsible carer' of a child under 13.

The claimant commitment will include details of the changes of circumstances that you must report, and the possible sanctions if you do not meet your 'work-related requirements'. The government intends that the claimant commitment will include how much you will be 'sanctioned' and how long a sanction will last. The government has said that it also expects the claimant commitment to include a summary of your rights.

There is more information about sanctions in Chapter 6.

EXAMPLE

The claimant commitment

Jenny is 32 and lives alone. She loses her job and claims universal credit. Her claimant commitment says that she understands that she must report any changes of circumstances relevant to her universal credit award. It also states that she must be available for full-time work and lists her personal circumstances that are relevant to her looking for work. There is a section about the type of work that she is looking for initially, and what she must do every week to look for work. It states that she has to attend the Jobcentre Plus office whenever she is asked to do so, and tells her about the sanctions that may apply if she does not meet these requirements. It explains her right of appeal if her universal credit is sanctioned.

How do you accept a claimant commitment?

There will be different ways in which you can accept a 'claimant commitment'. The government expects most people to use online methods, so the commitment will normally be in electronic form. However, the government plans there to be other ways of agreeing to the commitment, such as by telephone or in a face-to-face interview, if you need extra support.

Can you change your claimant commitment?

The government has said that you will be able to ask to change your 'claimant commitment' if your circumstances change, but the law does not say that you will have the right to do so. The government intends that changes will be made by discussion and negotiation with you, but the law gives the Department for Work and Pensions (DWP) the power to decide when and how your commitment is updated. The government intends that, if you are unhappy with what your claimant commitment says you must do to look for work, you will be able to ask for this to be reviewed by the DWP.

What CPAG says

Conditionality

CPAG has always welcomed the provision of support for benefit claimants to move into work if they are able to do so. However, the focus on the individual behaviour of claimants ignores the reality of an economy with few available jobs and where work is not a guaranteed route out of poverty.

The claimant commitment will be designed so that it sets out what work-related requirements a claimant has to meet. CPAG is concerned that the way in which the law has been written focuses on people complying with the rules, and that this is a missed opportunity to find a better way of engaging people in the process of moving towards work.

Another key concern is that it may become harder to challenge decisions effectively if there is not a clear set of rules setting out when people can and cannot be expected to take certain action. This is likely to impact most on vulnerable groups who may struggle to access advice and support to challenge decisions. Whatever the rules look like, it is vital that any decisions can be challenged by claimants on a level playing field, and without incurring significant costs.

If you cannot agree on what your commitment should say and you are 'sanctioned' (ie, the amount of your universal credit is reduced) because you do not meet its requirements, you can appeal.

There is more information about sanctions in Chapter 6 and more information about appeals in Chapter 7.

If you move into a different 'conditionality group' because of a change in your circumstances, you must have some of the requirements in your claimant commitment changed. If the decision maker does not accept that you should be in a different group, you may still have to appeal.

2. What are you expected to do?

There are four different 'conditionality groups', which describe what kind of things you are expected to do to move towards work. These requirements may also apply if you (or your partner) are working but your income is low.

What the law says

Conditionality groups

- The four conditionality groups are:
  - no work-related requirements
  - work-focused interviews
  - work-focused interviews and work preparation
  - all work-related requirements (this includes being available for and looking for work, as well as the other requirements above).

- You may have to attend an interview to discuss what you are doing to meet these requirements and provide evidence to show you have met them. You must report any changes of circumstances that are relevant to the group you should be in.

Sections 13 and 23 Welfare Reform Act 2012

Who helps you move towards work?

The government introduced a new initiative, called the Work Programme, in summer 2011. This is delivered by at least two 'prime' contractors in each region of the UK, who may then sub-contract other organisations to help you get work. If you are looking for work, you may still have to 'sign on' at the Jobcentre Plus office and may be referred to the Work Programme for further help.

Most people will not be immediately referred to the Work Programme. The government intends that, when you claim universal credit, you will have a named adviser in your local Jobcentre Plus office who will be responsible for helping you to meet your 'work-related requirements'.

In the longer term, the person helping you to look for or prepare for work (your 'personal adviser') may not be employed by the Department for Work and Pensions (DWP). Although this could be the person you see most often, the actual decisions about your universal credit entitlement, including whether it should be 'sanctioned', will still be made by a decision maker in the DWP. It is expected that your personal adviser will make recommendations to the decision maker.

What happens if you are claiming another benefit?

If you are claiming contributory employment and support allowance or contribution-based jobseeker's allowance as well as universal credit, you may also have to meet some of the new 'work-related requirements' for that benefit. However, the government may introduce regulations to say that you only have to meet one set of requirements, rather than one for each of the benefits that you are claiming.

When are your requirements waived or changed?

What the law says

Waiving the requirements

- Regulations may be made to treat you as having complied with any of the work-related requirements when you have not, in fact, done so.

- Regulations may also be made to treat you as having taken the action you are required to take when you have not, in fact, done so.

Section 25 Welfare Reform Act 2012

The government will have the power to decide that you do not have to meet any of the 'work-related requirements' outlined in this chapter. It has not said exactly how it intends to use this power, but intends that, in addition to the situations described in this chapter, regulations will specify certain groups of people who will have fewer or no work-related requirements. Box A shows some likely examples.

Alternatively, a decision maker may be able to decide that you do not have to meet particular work-related requirements if s/he believes this is appropriate.

As the introduction of universal credit approaches, there will be more detailed rules and guidance produced.

Box A

Groups who may have their work-related requirements waived or changed

The government intends that you will have no work-related requirements in the following situations.

- You are over the qualifying age for pension credit, but must claim universal credit because of your partner's age. The government has said that only the younger member of a couple in these circumstances will have any work-related requirements. There is more information about universal credit and older people in Chapter 9.

- You are a full-time apprentice (even if you earn below your 'conditionality threshold').

- You have adopted a child within the last year and you are her/his 'responsible carer'. The government intends that this will only apply if you are not a relative or foster carer of the child.

- You are heavily pregnant or your pregnancy has recently ended. It is expected that this will apply from 11 weeks before the baby is due until 15 weeks after your pregnancy ends.

- You work and you normally earn enough to be above your conditionality threshold but your earnings are now reduced. It is expected that this will apply if you are on maternity or paternity leave, are on strike, get statutory sick pay, have to attend court (including jury service) or are in prison.

The government has also said that if you are in one of the following groups, your work-related requirements will be different.

- If you are a foster carer, your only requirement will be to take part in 'work-focused interviews' until your youngest foster child turns 16. If you are in a couple, this will normally only apply to one of you.

- If you are a 'family and friends carer' or a 'kinship carer', the government intends to introduce special rules to change your work-related requirements, although there are currently no detailed plans on this.

Which conditionality group are you in?

The remaining sections of this chapter explain the different 'conditionality groups'. Use the table on page 73 to identify the group you are likely to be in. Remember that your partner may be in a different group to you.

What CPAG says

Conditionality

The idea of an adviser having the discretion to adapt the rules to individual circumstances is potentially a good one. However, CPAG believes that this will not be a truly positive change unless advisers can develop a meaningful knowledge of people as individuals. Whether or not the right decisions are made will depend on discussing a particular situation and all the relevant circumstances. This will be harder to achieve if advisers are under pressure to see more people in less time. Investment in the people who will help claimants move towards work is therefore needed.

Which conditionality group are you in?

Group	Work-related requirements
You are caring for a severely disabled person	No work-related requirements
You have 'limited capability for work-related activity'	
You are a lone parent or the responsible carer of a child under one	
You earn above a certain amount (your 'conditionality threshold')	
You are a full-time apprentice	
You have recently experienced domestic violence	
You are a lone parent or the responsible carer of a child aged one or two	Work-focused interviews
You are a single or 'nominated' foster carer	
You are a lone parent or the responsible carer of a child aged three or four	Normally work-focused interviews, but possibly work preparation in the future
You have 'limited capability for work'	Work preparation and work-focused interviews
You are a jobseeker, or you are not in one of the above groups	All work-related requirements
You are doing some work, but are not in one of the above groups	

3. Who has no work-related requirements?

In certain circumstances, you cannot be asked to undertake any 'work-related requirements' to get universal credit.

What the law says

No work-related requirements

- You do not have any work-related requirements if you have regular and substantial caring responsibilities for a severely disabled person.

- You do not have any work-related requirements if you are a lone parent or the responsible carer of a child under the age of one.

- You do not have any work-related requirements if you have limited capability for work-related activity.

- You do not have any work-related requirements if you are a recent victim of domestic violence.

- You do not have any work-related requirements if your household income (including that of your partner if you have one) is above your conditionality threshold.

- There may be other circumstances when you do not have any work-related requirements.

Sections 19 and 24(5) and (6) Welfare Reform Act 2012

Are you caring for a severely disabled person?

You will have no 'work-related requirements' if you get a carer's addition in your universal credit. You get this addition if you care for a severely disabled person for at least 35 hours a week.

The definition of who is a 'severely disabled person' has not yet been decided. However, for carer's allowance, this is linked to the rate of disability living allowance or attendance allowance received by the person being cared for. All disability living allowance claimants between the ages of 16 and 64 will be transferred to a new benefit called personal independence payment from 2013 onwards. This may affect your work-related requirements if the person for whom you care is transferred to personal independence payment, as it has not yet been decided which rates of this benefit will mean that s/he counts as a severely disabled person.

There is more information about universal credit and carers in Chapter 9.

Are you caring for a child under one?

If you have a child under one included as part of your family in your universal credit award and you are a lone parent or the 'responsible carer' in a couple, you will have no 'work-related requirements'. Couples will be able to decide jointly who is the responsible carer of a child. If you cannot agree, you will probably both have some work-related requirements. There may be regulations to allow the Department for Work and Pensions to decide for you if you disagree about who is the responsible carer.

EXAMPLE

The responsible carer

Luis and Patricia have a joint claim for universal credit. When their son Pablo is born, they nominate Patricia as the responsible carer. She has no work-related requirements, and Luis is looking for work. Patricia is offered a job when Pablo is six months old. She cannot take the job unless there is someone else to look after Pablo, so the couple decide to nominate Luis as the responsible carer instead. The decision maker agrees and Luis no longer has to look for work. Patricia is able to take the job while Luis looks after Pablo.

As you and your partner can jointly nominate the responsible carer, you will also be able to change who this person is. The government intends that this will be possible after a certain period of time (perhaps a year) or if the decision maker accepts that there has been a relevant change in your household circumstances.

Do you have 'limited capability for work-related activity'?

The severity of your health problem or disability will be decided by using a test designed to identify whether your illness or disability is so serious that you should not be expected to prepare for a return to work at the moment.

There is more information about this test in Chapter 4.

Have you recently experienced domestic violence?

Even if you would normally have to meet some or all of the 'work-related requirements', you will not have to do so for 13 weeks if you have experienced domestic violence. The government intends that you must no longer live with the perpetrator and that you must have evidence from a professional that the abuse is likely to have occurred. You will also have to request that your work-related requirements are suspended within six months of the incident.

It is likely that the definition of domestic violence will be that you have experienced actual or threatened physical, emotional or sexual abuse and that the perpetrator was your partner or a relative.

Do you earn above a certain amount?

Once you (and your partner if you have one) have more than a certain amount of earnings, you will not be expected to look for more work. This is called the 'conditionality threshold'. The government has said that the threshold will be set at the amount you would earn if you worked the number of hours that your 'claimant commitment' says you must be available for work and you were paid at the national minimum wage. The threshold will be based on your gross earnings, before deducting any tax and national insurance contributions that you must pay.

If you live with your partner, your conditionality threshold will be based on your joint income. It will be the total amount you would earn if you both worked the number of hours that you must be available for work and were paid the minimum wage.

If your joint income is above your conditionality threshold, it does not matter how much you each earn individually. If your joint income is below the threshold, normally you will both be expected to look for work. However, if you already work full time, but your partner does not, you will not have to look for more work, but your partner will.

EXAMPLE

The conditionality threshold

Bob and Derek claim universal credit as a couple. They have no children or health problems, and no savings or other income. They are both over 21, so the minimum wage they would get is £6.08 an hour. Their joint conditionality threshold is 35 hours multiplied by £6.08, multiplied by two (as they are both expected to look for full-time work). This is £425.60 a week.

A month later, Derek finds a job. He works 40 hours a week and receives £350 a week before tax and national insurance. They are still below their conditionality threshold, so Bob must still be available for and looking for full-time work. However, if he finds a job paying £76 a week or more, the couple's earnings will be above their joint conditionality threshold and they will then have no work-related requirements.

If your earnings vary, regulations will say how these will be averaged to decide whether or not they are above the conditionality threshold. There will also be regulations to allow your earnings to be treated as above your conditionality threshold if you are employed and normally earn above this amount but your earnings have decreased because, for example, you are on sick or maternity leave. The conditionality threshold will also apply if you are self-employed and your earnings are low.

There is more information about how your earnings are likely to be calculated if you are self-employed in Chapter 4.

4. Who must take part in work-focused interviews?

If it is accepted that you are unlikely to move into work soon, you may only have to take part in 'work-focused interviews' and have no other 'work-related requirements' as a condition of getting universal credit. You are most likely to be in this group if you look after young children or if you are a foster carer.

What the law says

Work-focused interviews

- You must take part in work-focused interviews if you are a lone parent or the responsible carer of a child aged one or two. If the child is three or four, you may also have to prepare for work in the future.

- Regulations will specify other groups of people who must take part in work-focused interviews.

- Regulations will outline the purpose of interviews. They will focus on making it more likely that you move into work, work more hours or get a better paid job. The Department for Work and Pensions decides what it means to participate, including when and where the interviews take place.

Sections 15, 20 and 21 Welfare Reform Act 2012

What happens at a work-focused interview?

You may have already attended a 'work-focused interview' for a benefit you or your partner are currently claiming.

The purpose of the interviews for universal credit will be to discuss how you can remain in or obtain work, including getting more work if you work already. Specific topics are likely to include those listed in Box B.

Box B
What will be discussed at a work-focused interview?

Likely subjects to be discussed at a work-focused interview include:

- your qualifications and training
- any medical condition or disability which may be a barrier to working
- your caring or childcare responsibilities and how they affect your ability to move into work
- potential work and training opportunities for the future, including the option of self-employment
- how universal credit will make you better off in work
- accessing help and support to assist you to move into work

Note: the above list is based on the rules on work-focused interviews for current benefits.

The regulations for employment and support allowance were changed in 2011 to make it clear that a work-focused interview is not necessarily a face-to-face meeting and can take place by phone. Regulations for universal credit will say what you have to do to take part in the interview and are likely to be based on the rules for employment and support allowance. In order to take part, you must take part in discussions and provide any information requested.

Are you a foster carer?

The government has said that there will be special rules for registered foster carers who have a child placed with them. If you are a single foster carer or the 'responsible carer' in a couple, you will only have to attend 'work-focused interviews' until your youngest foster child is 16. Your partner will normally have the 'work-related requirements' that are appropriate for her/him.

If your foster child has extra care needs, you may not have to look for work until s/he is 18.

If both you and your partner need to care full time for your foster child because of the level of her/his extra needs, you and your partner may only have to attend work-focused interviews and will have no other work-related requirements.

If you are between placements, you will not have any additional work-related requirements for the first eight weeks after the last placement ended, provided you intend to continue fostering.

Are you caring for a child under five?

The government intends that, initially, all lone parents and 'responsible carers' of young children who are at least one year old but have not yet started school must attend 'work-focused interviews', but they will not have to prepare for work as well. The law allows the government to decide in the future that if you are in this situation and your youngest child is three or four, you will also have to prepare for work, but it does not currently plan to use this power.

EXAMPLE

Work-focused interviews

Anwar is the responsible carer for his daughter Aisha. She is four and goes to nursery for three hours every weekday morning. Anwar has to drop her off and pick her up, but he is able to work two hours a day during the time Aisha is at nursery. He has spoken to his manager and is confident that he can increase his hours once Aisha starts school. He explains his situation at a work-focused interview and it is accepted that he does not need to prepare further for work at the moment. He must still take part in work-focused interviews when asked to do so.

If Anwar's employer thought he needed to do more training to be ready to increase his working hours, Anwar could discuss this with his personal adviser at an interview to see if there was any help available to do this.

5. Who must prepare for work?

Some people must prepare for work by taking some of the action discussed in their 'work-focused interviews', but they are not expected to look for or take a job.

What the law says

Preparing for work

• You are required to prepare for work if you have limited capability for work, but do not have limited capability for work-related activity.

• You may also be required to prepare for work if you are a lone parent or responsible carer of a child age three or four (but currently there are no plans to introduce these rules).

• Regulations may state which other groups of people must prepare for work.

• Work preparation can include spending a set amount of time on activities including:
  – having a skills assessment
  – improving your personal presentation
  – doing training
  – participating in the Work Programme
  – doing work experience or work placements
  – developing your own business plan
  – undertaking a work-focused health-related assessment if you have limited capability for work.

• Other activities may be added to the above list if your adviser thinks it necessary.

Sections 16 and 21 Welfare Reform Act 2012

What does 'limited capability for work' mean?

'Limited capability for a work' is a test of whether your health or disability means you are not currently able to work. It is currently used to decide whether you qualify for employment and support allowance and will be used to decide whether you qualify for an additional amount of universal credit.

There is more information about this test in Chapter 4.

It is not clear whether you will have to look for work if it is decided that you do not have limited capability for work and you have appealed against the decision because you disagree with it.

How must you prepare for work?

The rules for preparing for work are similar to those that have already been introduced for most people who claim employment and support allowance. If you have to prepare for work, you must also take part in 'work-focused interviews' if asked to do so.

EXAMPLE

Preparing for work

Thomas has been claiming employment and support allowance as he has bipolar disorder which means he is unable to work. He has limited capability for work when he is transferred to universal credit and so must prepare for work. Thomas used to work in an office, but is worried that his knowledge of computing will not be good enough to get a similar job when he is able to return to work.

He attends a work-focused interview and agrees with his personal adviser that he will attend a two-month computing course to update his skills. His adviser agrees to look for a one-week work placement after the course ends, so he can see how well he copes with being at work. A separate assessment of how his mental health will affect his ability to manage a job is arranged by the adviser.

People with poor health may also have to have a 'work-focused health-related assessment'. This will look at how your health could make it difficult to work and what could be done to overcome this. These assessments were introduced in 2008 for employment and support allowance, but then scrapped in 2011. The government has said that they will be a part of the new Work Programme, but they are currently not mentioned in any regulations.

There may be new rules on how much time you must spend preparing for work. It is possible that there will be an overall time each week that you must spend, or that the amount of time will be linked to particular activities suggested by your personal adviser.

What do you not have to do?
If you must prepare for work, you will not have to look for, apply for or take a job, as these are different 'work-related requirements'. However, you could be expected to do work experience or take a placement with an employer. The current regulations for employment and support allowance say that you cannot be told to have any sort of medical treatment as a way of preparing for work. It is possible that this will also be the case for universal credit.

The current employment and support allowance regulations allow you to restrict your work preparation hours to your child's school hours if s/he is 12 or under. This should also apply to lone parents and 'responsible carers' with 'limited capability for work' who are claiming universal credit.

6. Who must look for work?

Anyone who is not in one of the first three 'conditionality groups' (listed on page 69) must look for work. This involves being 'available for work' and 'actively seeking work'.

What the law says

Looking for work

- If you have all the work-related requirements, you must be available for work and actively looking for work – ie, you must do anything reasonable to find a job.

- To look for work, you may have to spend a specific amount of time:
  - carrying out work searches
  - applying for particular jobs
  - maintaining an online profile
  - registering with an employment agency
  - seeking references.

- You may be able to limit the work you will look for or accept, either temporarily or permanently, by the:
  - type of work
  - number of hours
  - wages
  - location.

- In general, you must be willing and able to start work immediately, although this rule may be relaxed for some people.

Sections 17, 18 and 22 Welfare Reform Act 2012

What does 'actively looking for work' mean?

If you have all the 'work-related requirements', you will be expected to do the same sort of things that are expected from people currently claiming jobseeker's allowance. There is a general requirement that you must do anything 'reasonable' to help you find work and there are specific requirements in addition to this. Regulations are likely to say that you must spend the number of hours that your 'claimant commitment' says you should be available for work actually looking for work.

The government intends to introduce regulations to say that if you do anything to sabotage your own work search (such as being violent or abusive in interviews or spoiling job applications), this will not count towards your activity for that week. These rules are similar to those that already exist for jobseeker's allowance.

EXAMPLE

Actively looking for work

Samantha has been claiming universal credit and looking for work for over six months. At a meeting to discuss Samantha's work-related requirements, her personal adviser decides that she needs to think about doing a training course to make her more attractive to employers.

Samantha has an interview about a training opportunity that her personal adviser arranges for her, and the interviewer gets in touch with the Jobcentre Plus office to say that he thought she was rude and unco-operative during the interview. The interview does not count towards meeting her work-related requirements for that week, and she may be sanctioned.

The requirement to spend a specified amount of time each week looking for work is a new one. This is expected to be part of your claimant commitment. It is also possible that your claimant commitment will state that you should undertake one specific activity or apply for a particular job.

What does 'being available for work' mean?

The current definition of 'being available for work' is that you are willing and able to take up full-time work. This is usually defined as over 40 hours a week for jobseeker's allowance, but the government has suggested that it might be 35 hours for universal credit. You will probably be expected to accept a part-time job if you are offered one. You must normally be able to take up work immediately, and take any job that pays at least the minimum wage which is within 90 minutes travel time of where you live. Special rules will allow you to restrict your availability for work in certain circumstances.

Do you have a good work history?

Currently, for jobseeker's allowance, if you have been in work recently you may be able to restrict the type of work you are seeking for up to 13 weeks. This includes both the type of job and the level of pay. This will also apply to universal credit, although the decision to allow you to restrict the sort of work that you are looking for will be at the discretion of your personal adviser. How your personal adviser will decide whether or not you have a 'good work history', which will allow you to limit the jobs you look for, is outlined in Box C.

Box C
Do you have a good work history?

Whether or not you can restrict the type of job you are looking for depends on:

- the length of time you were employed in the same occupation
- how long it has been since your last job ended
- your skills and qualifications
- training you have done for the job
- the availability of the type of job you used to do
- your prospects of getting the same kind of job you used to have

Do you have childcare responsibilities?

The government has said that, if you are a lone parent or 'responsible carer' of a child under 13, you may limit your availability for work to your child's normal school hours. You will also be able to place limitations based on the time needed to take your child to and from school, and any necessary arrangements for the school holidays. A couple will not have to nominate a responsible carer and you can instead share childcare responsibilities, provided you are looking for the equivalent of one full-time job and another job during your child's school hours between the two of you. Both of you must also have a reasonable chance of finding a job.

As some children start school after their fifth birthday, the government has said that (for jobseeker's allowance) if you are a lone parent, you will be treated as available for work if your youngest child is five and has not started school, provided alternative childcare arrangements are not available. The government has not said that this will also apply to universal credit, but it has said that the rules for jobseeker's allowance and universal credit will be as similar as possible, so this may also apply.

If you sometimes look after your child who normally lives with your ex-partner, you may be able to place some restrictions on your availability for work. This will depend on when you look after your child and her/his age.

Do you have a disability or health problems?

If you do not meet the conditions for having 'limited capability for work', but have a disability or poor health for which you are having regular treatment, you may be able to restrict your availability for work. You will have to provide evidence of how your condition or treatment limits the type, location or hours of work for which you are available. If accepted, this will also limit the hours you must spend looking for work. **Note:** the government may still decide to set a minimum number of hours that you must be available for work.

You will also be able to 'self-certify' yourself as temporarily sick and unable to look for work. The government intends that you will only be able to do this twice a year, and only for up to seven days.

Do you care for a disabled person?

If you do not meet the conditions for a carer's addition (which would mean you have no 'work-related requirements'), but you care for a disabled person, you will be able to restrict your availability for work. You will only have to be available for work that does not interfere with your caring responsibilities.

Note: the government may still decide to set a minimum number of hours that you must be available for work.

Do you have to be available for work immediately?

As is the case for jobseeker's allowance, you will normally be expected to start work or attend a job interview immediately. Box D lists some planned exceptions to this rule.

Box D
Who does not need to be immediately available to attend an interview or start work?

- If you are doing voluntary work, you are given 48 hours' notice to attend an interview and a week's notice to start paid work.

- You are given a 'reasonable time' if you need to arrange childcare before you can attend an interview or start work.

- If you are signed off as sick by your doctor, you do not have to be available to start work until your medical certificate expires.

- If you have a job, you are not expected to be available for other work until you have served your notice period.

Do you already have a job?

If you work fewer hours than your 'claimant commitment' says you must be available for work, you will be expected to spend the rest of that time looking for more work, unless you are already earning sufficient to be above your 'conditionality threshold'. This could be more work for your current employer, a second job in addition to your current one, or a different job with better pay. If you decide to focus on only one of these options, you must have a reasonable prospect of success.

Similarly, if you are self-employed, the government intends that you can choose to try to increase your earnings from your self-employment. If this is unsuccessful, it is likely that you will then be expected to look for a job as well.

Any 'work-related requirements' that you must meet will fit around your existing job. You will not have to be available to attend an interview immediately if you are at work at the time.

You will not be expected to give up a permanent job for better paid, temporary work. Your personal adviser will also take into account your other circumstances – eg, if your current job allows you to work flexibly because you have caring responsibilities.

If you change jobs but your earnings are still below your conditionality threshold, you may be allowed time to settle into your new job before you must start looking for more work. This may also apply if you start a job after being unemployed. The government has not said how long this will last, or whether the job you start must be for a certain number of hours.

The government intends that if you are on maternity or paternity leave from your job, you will not have any work-related requirements during this period.

Are there any other special circumstances?

There will be other special circumstances in which you will not have to look for work. The government intends these to include time when you have to attend court (including when you are on jury service, appearing as a witness or serving as a justice of the peace) and if you are in prison.

The government intends that your personal adviser will be able to decide that you do not have any other 'work-related requirements' while you are on a compulsory training course if s/he accepts that this is reasonable given the amount of time you must spend on the course.

There will also be situations when your personal adviser will be able to reduce or stop your work-related requirements temporarily if s/he thinks this is appropriate. The government intends these to include situations when:

- you have undertaken all the activity that is reasonable to expect of you in a particular week, but you have not spent the amount of time your 'claimant commitment' says you must spend looking for work
- you are doing voluntary work, provided you are still trying to find paid work
- there is a domestic emergency
- a relative or close friend has recently died

What CPAG says

Conditionality

As an alternative to work-related requirements, CPAG supports the idea of a 'personal budget' for moving towards work, which a claimant would decide how to spend in discussion with an adviser. Larger budgets could be allocated to people with health problems, a disability or caring responsibilities, in recognition of the extra barriers to work they face. This system would allow the adviser to work with claimants, rather than dictating what they should do. It would also mean that the services that people use would be the right ones for their individual circumstances.

CPAG believes that an alternative personal budget system would require less public money to be spent on administration (particularly as it is likely there would be fewer sanctions, hardship payments and appeals). These savings could then be used to overcome the structural barriers to work that exist in our society. Just two of the many potential areas of investment are better funding for childcare and ensuring that schemes such as Access to Work give disabled people true equality in the labour market.

Further information

There is more information on conditionality requirements for current benefits and 'work-focused interviews' in CPAG's *Welfare Benefits and Tax Credits Handbook*.

Chapter 6
Sanctions and fines

This chapter covers:

1. When can your universal credit be sanctioned?

2. When is your universal credit not sanctioned?

3. How much is a sanction and how long does it last?

4. When can you get hardship payments?

5. When can you be fined?

6. What happens to your universal credit after a benefit offence?

What you need to know

- If you or your partner do not meet the conditions in your 'claimant commitment', the amount of your universal credit can be reduced. This is called being 'sanctioned'. The amount of the sanction depends on what happened. The sanction lasts for a set period of time. You should not be sanctioned if you have a good reason for acting as you did.

- If you have been sanctioned, you may be able to get a reduced payment of universal credit. This is called a 'hardship payment'. This may be a loan, which you must repay from your future universal credit.

- If you have been overpaid universal credit because you failed to provide information or gave incorrect information, you may be given a fine. This is called a 'civil penalty'.

- If you have given false information or made an error that is serious enough for the government to think there are grounds to prosecute you for fraud, you may be given the option to accept a fine instead of being prosecuted. You can be given this kind of fine, which is called a 'penalty as an alternative to prosecution', even if you are not actually overpaid.

- If you are convicted of a benefit offence or you accept a fine to avoid being prosecuted, your universal credit will be stopped or reduced for a set period of time.

1. When can your universal credit be sanctioned?

If you do not meet your 'work-related requirements', your universal credit can be reduced. This is called a 'sanction'.

Do you have to look for work?

The most severe sanctions will only apply to you if you must look for work, and for what the government believes are the most serious failures. The law is currently being changed to make the jobseeker's allowance rules on sanctions more like the ones that will apply to universal credit.

- The most serious sanctions can be imposed if you do not apply for a particular job or take up a job offer, do not take up a mandatory work placement, or you give up your job or lose pay.

- You can be sanctioned if you do not take a job you are offered, if you lose your job, or if your earnings decrease *before* you claim universal credit. The law does not give a time limit on how long before you claim universal credit these things must have happened. The government intends that, if the length of time that you would have been sanctioned for has already passed before you claim universal credit, you will not receive a sanction. It is also planned that you will not be sanctioned under this rule if more than 26 weeks have passed before you claim.

- You can be sanctioned if it is decided that you are not 'available for work' or 'actively looking for work'.

- You can also be sanctioned if you do not undertake any of your other 'work-related requirements', in the same way as people who do not have to look for work.

What the law says

When sanctions apply

- You can be given a 'higher level sanction' if you are expected to look for work and:
  - you do not take up a work placement
  - you do not apply for a specific job
  - you do not take up an offer of a job
  - you stop work or lose pay, either voluntarily or as a result of your misconduct.

- Your universal credit can still be sanctioned if you did not take up an offer of a job, or you stopped work or lost pay either voluntarily or as a result of your misconduct, before you claimed universal credit.

- If you work and earn sufficient to be above your conditionality threshold and so do not have to look for more work, you can be given a higher level sanction if you give up your job or lose pay and this means you then have to look for more work. This only applies if you have acted voluntarily or if the situation has arisen from your own misconduct.

- If you do not meet any of your work-related requirements, do not participate in an interview to discuss them or do not report a relevant change of circumstances, you can be sanctioned.

- If your failure is something for which you cannot receive a higher level sanction, you may still receive a sanction if you do not have good reason for your actions. The law refers to these type of sanctions as 'other sanctions'.

- Regulations may say that sanctions can be suspended, terminated, or not imposed at all in particular cases.

- Sanctions on a previous award of universal credit or another benefit may also apply if you reclaim universal credit at a later date.

Sections 26 and 27 Welfare Reform Act 2012

EXAMPLE

Sanctions if you must look for work

Mandy lives alone and has no health problems. She gives up her job because she finds it boring. Two weeks later, she has not found work and she claims universal credit. The decision maker at the Department for Work and Pensions does not accept that she had a good reason for leaving her job and decides that her universal credit will be sanctioned for 13 weeks. The sanction period starts from the date she gave up her job.

Do you *not* have to look for work?

Your universal credit can be sanctioned if you do not do any of the things outlined in your 'claimant commitment'.

- If you do not take up a work placement that you have been told to do, you can be sanctioned. (**Note:** the sanction for this is less serious than it would be if you had to look for work.)

- If you do not undertake any of the activities that you are required to do to prepare for work, you can be sanctioned.

- If you do not take part in a 'work-focused interview', you can be sanctioned.

- If you do not take part in an interview to discuss your 'work-related requirements', you can be sanctioned.

- If you do not report a relevant change in your circumstances, you can be sanctioned.

EXAMPLE

Sanctions if you do not report a change of circumstances

Boris and Sonya claim universal credit as a couple. Sonya's daughter from her first marriage, Rhea, normally lives with them. She is three, so Sonya only has to attend work-focused interviews.

Rhea goes to live full time with her father. As Sonya no longer looks after Rhea, she is now expected to look for work. If she does not immediately tell the Jobcentre Plus office about the change in her circumstances, she may be sanctioned. She may also be overpaid universal credit if she does not report that her daughter no longer lives with her.

2. When is your universal credit not sanctioned?

In most cases, your universal credit will not be reduced (ie, you will not receive a 'sanction') if you can show that you had a 'good reason' for acting as you did.

What the law says

When sanctions do not apply

- If you leave work or lose pay as a result of your misconduct and you are expected to look for work, you can always be sanctioned. Regulations may define what 'misconduct' means.

- In any other situation, you will not be sanctioned if you can show that you acted with 'good reason'.

- If you have left your job or lost pay, you can only be sanctioned if you acted 'voluntarily'. Regulations may define what 'voluntarily' means.

Sections 26 and 27 Welfare Reform Act 2012

In the current benefit rules, sanctions do not apply if you have 'good cause' and 'just cause' for your actions. The government intends not to have a detailed description of what counts as a good cause. Instead, the decision maker at the Department for Work and Pensions will consider all your circumstances and will have the discretion to decide whether you have a 'good reason'. When making this decision, the decision maker is likely to use information from your personal adviser, as s/he may have referred you for a decision on whether you should be sanctioned.

Box A
Do you have a good reason?

The following factors may be relevant when deciding whether or not you have a good reason for acting as you did:

- your physical and mental health
- transport difficulties
- your understanding of the 'work-related requirement', especially if you were given misleading information, or if you have language or literacy problems
- a job interview or medical appointment which clashed with the work-related requirement and which could not be rearranged
- caring responsibilities
- a sudden illness or bereavement
- the high cost of any childcare needed to allow you to undertake the work-related requirement
- being outside the UK

The above list is based on the current definitions of 'good cause' and 'just cause' for jobseeker's allowance and employment and support allowance.

EXAMPLE

Good reason

Terry is made redundant after doing the same job for 15 years. At an interview just after he claims universal credit, his personal adviser suggests that he should apply for a similar job with a different employer, which is being advertised through the jobcentre. Terry agrees to do this, as it sounds like a good opportunity.

Before applying, Terry contacts the employer for more details. The job is not based at the main office, which would mean Terry would be working a long way from home. He would have to travel for about two hours to get to work, and the train and bus fares would cost him almost half of the salary on offer. Terry explains this to his personal adviser and it is accepted that he has a good reason for not applying for the job.

Have you left work or lost earnings voluntarily or because of misconduct?

The current jobseeker's allowance rules do not treat you as having left work voluntarily if you have been made redundant. This applies even if you took voluntary redundancy. The government intends that this will also apply to universal credit, so you should not be sanctioned if you have been made redundant. The government also intends that you will not be sanctioned if you leave the armed forces, even if you left voluntarily.

If you have been laid off or put on short-time working by your employer, you should not be sanctioned for losing pay if you continue to meet your employer's conditions.

If your employer ends your contract or changes it significantly without your agreement, you may be able to argue that you have not left work 'voluntarily'. This may also apply if you resign to avoid being dismissed from your job (although if this happens, it could be decided that your own misconduct was the cause of your leaving).

The government intends the words 'voluntarily' and 'misconduct' to mean what they do ordinarily, on a day-to-day basis, although it is possible that regulations will define them in particular circumstances.

Box B
What is 'misconduct'?

- Being careless or negligent might be misconduct if it is serious enough.

- Misconduct must normally be connected with your employment in some way, although it does not necessarily need to happen while you are working.

- Dishonesty is clearly misconduct if it means that your employer does not trust you and dismisses you because of this.

- Being persistently late or being off sick without explaining the situation to your employer might be misconduct.

- Refusing to work overtime might be misconduct if it is in your contract and the request was reasonable.

- If you resign to avoid being dismissed, this can count as misconduct.

- If you refuse to do something at work, this might be misconduct if you understood the instruction and do not have a good reason for refusing.

- If your employer says you were dismissed because of misconduct, but is really just reducing staff numbers, this should not count as misconduct.

- If you are dismissed for poor performance, this is not necessarily misconduct.

The above is based on previous decisions about unemployment benefit and jobseeker's allowance.

3. How much is a sanction and how long does it last?

The government has set out detailed plans of how it thinks sanctions will work in universal credit. However, there is currently very little detail in the law itself.

What the law says

Length of sanctions

- The maximum length of a 'higher level sanction' is three years.

- 'Other sanctions' can last:
  - until you meet a requirement (called a 'compliance condition')
  - for a fixed time, up to a maximum of 26 weeks
  - a combination of both of these.

- The length of a sanction depends on the number of times you have failed to do something within a given time.

- Regulations will set the amount of sanctions.

Sections 26(6) and (7) and 27(4), (5) and (8) Welfare Reform Act 2012

How much is a sanction?

The government has said that the most your universal credit will be reduced by will be the amount of the adult 'standard allowance'. In 2012/13, this is £71 a week for a single person and £111.45 for a couple. If you are single, you will normally lose all of your standard allowance if you are sanctioned. If you are in a couple, the government intends you to lose half of your standard allowance if one of you is sanctioned.

However, if your only 'work-related requirement' is to take part in 'work-focused interviews' and you fail to do this, your universal credit will be reduced by a percentage of your standard allowance. For your first failure, the government intends the reduction to be 20 per cent of your standard allowance if you are single and 10 per cent if you are in a couple. If you fail to attend more than one work-focused interview, the reduction will be doubled.

Your universal credit will be reduced by the same amount, even if you are working and receive a lower amount of universal credit because of your earnings. If the amount of your sanction is more than the amount of universal credit you normally receive, the government intends that your award will reduce to zero. The sanction will still last for the prescribed length of time.

The amount included in your universal credit to help cover your housing costs and the amounts included for your children will not be affected by a sanction if you are not working and you do not have any savings or other income.

How long does a sanction last?

If you must look for work, a sanction can last for up to three years. The most serious failures will be punished with a fixed-length sanction. These will be divided into 'high' and 'medium' level sanctions. You could also be given a 'low' level sanction in the same way as people who have to prepare for work.

You could be given a 'low' level sanction if you must prepare for work. A sanction will last until you comply with a 'work-related requirement' that you have failed to meet, and then for a set period afterwards. You can also be given a low level sanction to apply if you fail to report a relevant change in your circumstances that affects your work-related requirements. The length of your sanction will depend on how late you were in reporting the change.

Note: if you do not report a change of circumstances, you may also be overpaid and potentially prosecuted for fraud.

If your universal credit is sanctioned because you have not complied with a particular requirement (a 'compliance condition'), this will last until:

- you meet the original requirement
- you meet a new requirement that has replaced the original one
- you do something else that is accepted as being an equivalent work-related requirement

Regulations will say when you will be given a longer sanction for repeatedly not meeting your work-related requirements. If you fail to meet the same requirement within one year, the government intends that you will receive a longer sanction.

If you only need take part in 'work-focused interviews' and you fail to do so, the government intends that you will be sanctioned until you next take part in an interview.

EXAMPLE

Length of sanction

Jerry is expected to prepare for work. His universal credit has been sanctioned because he did not attend a training course his adviser found for him and he did not have a good reason for failing to attend. This is the first time Jerry has been sanctioned.

Jerry and his personal adviser agree that if he attends a different course, he will be treated as having met the original requirement and his sanction will end a week after he starts the course.

The current plans for how long sanctions will last are set out in the table below. If you have met your work-related requirements for at least one year, during which time you have been in work for at least six months at the level expected by your 'claimant commitment', the government intends that any outstanding sanctions will end.

Length of sanctions			
Sanctions if you must look for work			
What have you done wrong?	Length of sanction for first failure	Length of sanction for second failure within a year	Length of sanction for third failure within a year of second failure
Failed to apply for a job or take up a job offer without a good reason Left work or lost earnings voluntarily or because of misconduct Failed to attend a mandatory work placement	13 weeks (high level)	26 weeks (high level)	3 years (high level)
Failed to actively look for or be available for work	4 weeks (medium level)	13 weeks (medium level)	13 weeks (medium level)
Failed to undertake a specific work search activity Failed to attend an interview with your personal adviser or undertake other work-related activity	Until you comply and for one week after you do so (low level)	Until you comply and for two weeks after you do so (low level)	Until you comply and for four weeks after you do so (low level)

Sanctions if you must prepare for work

What have you done wrong?	Length of sanction for first failure	Length of sanction for second failure within a year	Length of sanction for third failure within a year of second failure
Failed to attend a work placement Failed to undertake work-related activity Failed to take part in a work-focused interview	Until you comply and for one week after you do so (low level)	Until you comply and for two weeks after you do so (low level)	Until you comply and for four weeks after you do so (low level)

Sanctions if you must only take part in work-focused interviews

What have you done wrong?	Length of sanction for first failure	Length of sanction for second and subsequent failures
Failed to take part in a work-focused interview	Until you take part in a work-focused interview (universal credit is reduced by 20% of adult standard allowance if you are single or by 10% if you are in a couple)	Until you take part in a work-focused interview (universal credit is reduced by 40% of adult standard allowance if you are single or 20% if you are in a couple)

What happens if your circumstances change?

If you have been sanctioned, the government intends the sanction period to continue even if your universal credit award ends. If you reclaim universal credit before the sanction period ends, the sanction continues for the rest of the period.

If you have been sanctioned as a single person and you then become part of a couple, the government intends the sanction to continue on your new couple claim. However, if your partner has been sanctioned and you separate, your new award of universal credit based on your being a single person will not be sanctioned.

The government intends to remove any sanction on your universal credit if you have undertaken all your 'work-related requirements' for one year, provided that during this time you have been in work at the level expected by your 'claimant commitment' for at least six months.

The government also intends to reduce the amount of an outstanding sanction to zero (ie, you will get your full universal credit entitlement) if you become unwell and are moved into the group with no work-related requirements because you are accepted as having a 'limited capability for work-related activity'. It intends that the sanction period will continue, so that if your health improves before the sanction period ends the sanction can start again.

EXAMPLE

Change of circumstances during a sanction

Leroy refuses to apply for a job that his personal adviser thinks is suitable for him because he believes the pay is inadequate for the type of work. This is not accepted as a good reason and his universal credit is sanctioned for 13 weeks. Two weeks after the sanction starts, he gets a job and the level of his salary means his universal credit award ends.

Five weeks after starting work, Leroy loses his job and reclaims universal credit. The decision maker sanctions his new award for the remaining six weeks of the sanction from his previous claim.

Note that Leroy could have appealed against the decision to sanction his award and argued that he had a good reason for not applying for the job. He may still be able to make a late appeal against the decision to sanction his universal credit.

What CPAG says

Sanctions

CPAG does not agree with tougher sanctions for people who do not comply with the imposed conditionality requirements.

There is little evidence that sanctions are an effective way to get people into sustainable jobs, or to reduce poverty rates overall. Furthermore, sanctions have been shown to have serious negative consequences. They are poorly understood by the people receiving them, who often do not know why their benefit has been reduced. They have a negative impact on health outcomes, and on poverty rates for individuals and families affected by them. Perhaps most worrying of all, research has shown that vulnerable groups are more likely to be sanctioned.

4. When can you get hardship payments?

If the amount of your universal credit is reduced because of a 'sanction', you may be able to qualify for 'hardship payments'. For some people, these payments may be made as loans and recovered from your award of universal credit.

What the law says

Hardship payments

- If a sanction is being used to reduce your universal credit award, additional payments may be made to you if you are 'in hardship'.

- Regulations will say:
    - when you are treated as being 'in hardship'
    - the other conditions you must meet
    - the amount of the payments
    - for how long payments are made
    - whether or not hardship payments are recoverable from you.

Section 28 Welfare Reform Act 2012

The government has said that the rules on who can get hardship payments will be similar to those that currently apply to jobseeker's allowance. This means that if you are in a 'vulnerable group', you may be able to get hardship payments straight away.

> ## Box C
> **Vulnerable groups**
>
> Under the current rules for jobseeker's allowance, a household is considered vulnerable if it has:
>
> * children
> * someone with a disability or a long-term medical condition
> * someone who is pregnant
> * someone with caring responsibilities
> * someone under 21 who was formerly 'looked after' by a local authority
> * an under 18-year-old able to claim universal credit

Even if you are in a vulnerable group, you will probably still need to show that you will face hardship if you are not awarded hardship payments. This is likely to mean that your other financial resources will be compared with the level of hardship payments you might get. The decision maker is also likely to consider the possibility that you will not be able to afford essential items, such as food, clothing, heating and accommodation.

In order to get hardship payments, you will have to provide details of your financial circumstances and continue to meet your 'work-related requirements'.

If you are not in a vulnerable group, there may be a period of time (a 'waiting period') before you can get any hardship payments, irrespective of your circumstances. For jobseeker's allowance, this waiting period is currently two weeks.

How much are hardship payments and how long do they last?

It is expected that 'hardship payments' will be a percentage of the amount by which your universal credit has been reduced. For example, the current rules for jobseeker's allowance say that, if you are single and have been sanctioned, you get 60 per cent of your normal amount if you are in hardship, or 80 per cent if you are seriously ill or pregnant. It is likely that similar amounts will be used for universal credit.

The government intends that if you are in a vulnerable group, you will be able to get hardship payments for the whole period of your sanction. However, if you are not in a 'vulnerable group', hardship payments might only be paid for a fixed period.

When are hardship payments recovered from you?

The government intends that some 'hardship payments' will be recoverable. It has not yet decided when or how they will be recovered. However, this is likely to be at the discretion of a decision maker, looking at all your circumstances, including whether you have children.

EXAMPLE

Hardship payments

Anita and Tony have two children, aged six and eight. Tony has just resigned from his job and the couple have claimed universal credit. Tony has been sanctioned for leaving his job without good reason. He is 'signing on' and looking for work. Anita is seven months pregnant and unwell because of complications in her pregnancy. The couple have no other income. They explain their circumstances to the decision maker and provide details of their finances. The decision maker decides that they can get hardship payments of universal credit immediately, and that these will not need to be repaid.

Note that Tony is also able to appeal against the decision to sanction his universal credit. He could argue that his wife's pregnancy and illness, together with the needs of their children, are good reasons for leaving his job (if this was why he stopped work).

5. When can you be fined?

If the information you give about your universal credit claim is not correct or up to date, you can be fined. The law sets out two different kinds of fine. If you give wrong or incomplete information and, as a result, you are overpaid, you can be given a fine called a 'civil penalty'.

If the Department for Work and Pensions thinks that you have deliberately given false information or if your error is more serious and it could prosecute you for fraud, you could be offered the option of a larger fine rather than being charged with an offence. The law calls this a 'penalty as an alternative to prosecution'.

Note: if you are being prosecuted for benefit fraud, have been offered a fine to avoid possibly being prosecuted, or have been invited to attend a formal interview, you should seek advice immediately.

How much is the fine?

The government intends the amount of a 'civil penalty' fine to be £50. The fine will be the same, even if you are only overpaid a small amount of universal credit. The government intends that if your overpayment is below a set amount (the most recent figure mentioned is £65), you will not be fined unless the Department for Work and Pensions (DWP) thinks that it could prosecute you.

If you accept a fine to avoid possibly being prosecuted for fraud, the amount of the fine will be more. You can also be fined even if you have not been overpaid at all.

There is more information about how overpayments happen and how they are calculated in Chapter 7.

When can you be fined?

What the law says

Civil penalties

- A civil penalty can be added to an overpayment of universal credit if the overpayment was caused by the fact that:
  - you negligently made an incorrect statement
  - you negligently provided incorrect information or evidence
  - you failed to report a relevant change of circumstances 'without reasonable excuse'.

- In the first two cases, you are not given a penalty if you have taken 'reasonable steps' to correct your error.

- These rules only apply if you have not been charged with an offence or been given a fine as an alternative to being prosecuted in connection with the overpayment.

Penalties as an alternative to prosecution

- If it appears to the DWP that there are grounds for prosecuting you for a benefit fraud offence, you can be offered one of the following instead:
  - a fine of £350, if there is no overpayment
  - a fine of 50 per cent of the amount of the recoverable overpayment, subject to a minimum of £350 and maximum of £2,000.

- The above amounts may be changed in the future.

- If you accept the fine, you cannot be prosecuted for that offence. You have 14 days after accepting the fine in which to change your mind and withdraw your acceptance. If you withdraw your acceptance, the DWP must refund any of the fine you have already paid, but may decide to prosecute you.

Sections 113, 114, 115 and 116 Welfare Reform Act 2012

The government has said that 'civil penalty' fines are designed to make sure you take proper care when claiming universal credit. Decision makers will have discretion about when you are fined under these rules and will decide whether you have been 'negligent' or have taken 'reasonable steps' to correct an error. For example, you might not be given a fine at all if you have a mental health problem and you did not understand what you were doing, even if you have been overpaid.

Civil penalty fines are similar to penalties that already exist for tax credits and the rules use similar terms. The factors taken into account in the tax credits guidance to decide whether or not to give you a penalty may also apply to universal credit.

Box D
Have you been negligent or do you have a reasonable excuse?

The decision on whether you have been negligent or have a reasonable excuse may be based on your individual circumstances, and how a careful person would act in your situation. This includes:

- your experience in dealing with financial matters
- your access to support, guidance or advice
- your health and wellbeing, including the impact of a disability

The above is based on current guidance for tax credits penalties.

You will be able to appeal against a decision to give you a civil penalty fine. The most likely grounds for your appeal will be that you did not act negligently or that you had a reasonable excuse for not providing information earlier.

There is more information about appeals in Chapter 7.

If the DWP believes that it could prosecute you for fraud, the fine you are given is similar to the one you can get as an alternative to being prosecuted in the current benefit rules. This is explained in Box E.

Box E

Current financial penalties and cautions

At present, before the introduction of universal credit, you can be cautioned instead of being prosecuted. You can also be given a fine of 30 per cent of the overpayment. You can only be cautioned or fined if you have actually been overpaid.

Cautions and fines are offered at a special interview. You must already have been interviewed under caution to get more information about why the DWP suspects you of fraud, and then have a separate interview with a different person to caution you formally, or offer you a fine instead of being prosecuted.

The rules for most other benefits will be changed to bring them into line with universal credit. The DWP will no longer use cautions when dealing with benefit offences. However, it is not yet clear what will need to happen when you are offered a 'fine as an alternative to prosecution'. It may be that you will be interviewed, in a similar way to the current rules, or a new system of offering fines may be introduced.

EXAMPLE

Fines

Nigel works part time. His daughter Clara attends nursery while he works and he receives help towards the costs of childcare in his universal credit. Nigel decides he wants to spend more time with Clara, reorganises his work and reduces her childcare by a few hours a week. He forgets to inform the DWP of this change in his childcare costs until six weeks later. The decison maker decides that Nigel has been negligent, but that the situation is not sufficiently serious to prosecute him for fraud. Nigel's universal credit award is amended, an overpayment calculated and a £50 fine is added to it.

Note that Nigel can appeal against the decision to add a fine to his overpayment if he has a reasonable excuse for not informing the DWP earlier.

What happens if you accept a fine to avoid being prosecuted but later change your mind?

If you accept a fine to avoid possibly being prosecuted, you will have 14 days from agreeing to pay to change your mind and not accept it. If you change your mind within the time limit, any payments you have made should be refunded to you.

It may be difficult to decide what to do. On the one hand, if you accept a fine, you avoid prosecution. On the other hand, you will have to pay the fine and you will be disqualified from benefit for a period. You should always seek independent advice to help you decide.

EXAMPLE

Fine instead of a possible prosecution

Aaron claims universal credit for himself and his two children. Before any payment is made, his claim is turned down as the decision maker believes the children live with his ex-wife Maria, who already gets universal credit for them. Aaron has not provided any evidence of when the children stay with him. Even though no overpayment has been made to Aaron, the Department for Work and Pensions believes that he deliberately claimed for the children dishonestly in order get more benefit, and so he could be prosecuted for fraud. Rather than start proceedings, Aaron is offered the alternative of paying a £350 fine. He has 14 days in which to decide whether or not to accept it. He should seek advice.

Note that Aaron may also be able to argue that he can claim for the children, depending on their living arrangements. To be convicted, it must be proved that he knew he was not entitled to amounts of universal credit for them.

How do you pay a fine?

A fine will be recoverable from you by the same method as an overpayment.

There is more information about overpayments and how they are recovered in Chapter 7.

If you have a joint universal credit claim, the fine will be recovered from your joint award. It may also be recovered by other methods, from you or from your partner. The fine will not be imposed on your partner if s/he was unaware of your negligence or if s/he has a reasonable excuse for not providing the information needed.

If a fine is being recovered from you and the decision that you have been overpaid is later changed (eg, if your appeal against the decision is successful), the Department for Work and Pensions must refund any amount of the fine that you have already paid.

What CPAG says

Fines

While the popular perception is one of 'scroungers' taking what they know they are not entitled to, CPAG fears that fines may be offered to frightened vulnerable people, who have made an innocent mistake. It is particularly concerning that penalties are to be introduced when there is no question that a person has acted dishonestly, or when someone has not actually been overpaid.

6. When happens to your universal credit after a benefit offence?

If you are convicted of a benefit offence or you accept a fine to avoid possibly being prosecuted, your universal credit entitlement will be sanctioned for a set period of time. This usually means that you are paid less benefit but, in some cases, this can mean losing entitlement altogether. Although the law calls this a 'sanction', it is different from the sanctions imposed for not undertaking your 'work-related requirements'.

It is possible that any universal credit you are paid while sanctioned under these rules may be recovered from you in the future.

What the law says

Sanctions for benefit offences

- You will be sanctioned for a set period if you accept a penalty as an alternative to prosecution or if you are convicted of benefit fraud.

- If it is your first offence (and not a serious one), you will be sanctioned for 13 weeks if convicted, or for four weeks if you accept a penalty as an alternative to prosecution.

- If you are convicted of a second offence within five years of being sanctioned under these rules, you will be sanctioned for 26 weeks, or three years for a third offence.

- You will be sanctioned for three years if you have been convicted and you were overpaid at least £50,000.

- You will be sanctioned for three years if you are convicted and you have been sentenced to one year or longer in prison (including suspended sentences).

- You will be sanctioned for three years if you have committed fraud over a period of more than two years.

- For a serious offence, you will be sanctioned for three years if you are found guilty of conspiracy to defraud the social security system.

- Regulations may specify other circumstances when you may be sanctioned for three years or may change the length of any of these sanctions.

Sections 118 and 119, and Schedule 2 paragraphs 56-63 Welfare Reform Act 2012

EXAMPLE

Sanction for a benefit offence

Connor accepts a fine of 50 per cent of the amount of an overpayment of universal credit as an alternative to being prosecuted, after it was found that he had not declared the casual work he had been doing. As well as the fine, he is sanctioned for four weeks. He does not challenge this decision.

Eighteen months later, he is again found to have been working and not declaring his earnings and so has been overpaid universal credit again. This time, he is not offered a fine and is prosecuted and convicted of fraud. As well as having to repay the overpayment, he is charged court costs, given a suspended sentence and also disqualified from universal credit for 26 weeks. However, he receives some universal credit during this time as he has no other income, having lost his job after being convicted.

Further information

There is more information about some of the terms and rules mentioned in this chapter, including the definitions of 'good cause' and 'just cause' for jobseeker's allowance and employment and support allowance, and the current rules on fraud and financial penalties in CPAG's *Welfare Benefits and Tax Credits Handbook*.

Chapter 7
Problems with universal credit

This chapter covers:

1. What can you do if there is a problem with your universal credit?

2. What happens if you are overpaid?

3. What can you do if you disagree with a decision?

4. Making a complaint

What you need to know

- If you are overpaid universal credit, the Department for Work and Pensions (DWP) can recover it, even if its own mistake caused the overpayment.

- Decision makers have discretion not to recover an overpayment. They use a code of practice to help them decide.

- If the DWP decides to recover an overpayment, you do not have a right of appeal against this. However, you may be able to challenge the decision in other ways.

- The DWP usually recovers an overpayment from your ongoing award of universal credit, but may recover it in other ways, including from your earnings.

- With most decisions about universal credit, if you are unhappy, you can appeal to an independent tribunal. Before you do so, you will probably need to ask the DWP to consider revising the decision.

1. What can you do if there is a problem with your universal credit?

Various problems could arise with your universal credit award or payment. What you can do about the problem depends on what has gone wrong.

- If your circumstances have changed, you must report anything that might affect your benefit or any other change you are told to report. There is more information about changes in circumstances in Chapter 3.

- If you are told that you have been overpaid universal credit, you may have to repay it. First, you should check whether the overpayment is correct.

- If you are unhappy with your award, you can ask the Department for Work and Pensions (DWP) to change the decision, or you can appeal.

- If there is a delay in getting paid, you may be able to get a 'payment on account'. There is more information on these payments in Chapter 3.

- If your benefit is reduced because of a 'sanction', you may be able to ask the DWP to change the decision, or you can appeal. There is more information about sanctions in Chapter 6.

- If you are fined, you may be able to ask the DWP to change the decision, or you can appeal. There is more information about fines in Chapter 6.

2. What happens if you are overpaid?

If more universal credit is paid to you than you are entitled to, you have been overpaid.

What the law says

Overpayments

Any amount of universal credit paid in excess of your correct entitlement creates an overpayment.

Section 105 Welfare Reform Act 2012

There are many reasons why universal credit might be overpaid, including the following.

- You give the wrong information when you claim.

- You are late reporting a change of circumstances.

- Your employer gives the wrong details about your earnings or is late reporting these to HM Revenue and Customs (HMRC).

- The Department for Work and Pensions (DWP) makes a mistake when it works out your award or when it records information you give.

- The DWP does not act on information you give.

- The DWP does not pass on information from one department to another.

If your universal credit is overpaid, the DWP should do the following.

- **Change the decision.** If the overpayment is because of a change in your entitlement to universal credit, the DWP must 'revise' or 'supersede' the decision awarding you benefit. These are the legal ways in which the DWP can change a decision on your entitlement. Regulations will set out the circumstances in which the DWP does not have to change the decision before recovering an overpayment – eg, if you are paid twice by mistake or if someone else cashes a cheque intended for you.

- **Calculate the overpayment.** The DWP will calculate how much has been overpaid. Regulations will say how this will be done. It is likely that the DWP will work out what your entitlement should have been and only ask you to repay the difference. For example,

EXAMPLES

Why overpayments happen

Parveen is working part time. Her employer has mixed up the details of her earnings with those of someone else and has told HMRC that she earns less than she does. When the mistake comes to light, the DWP revises her award. She has an overpayment of universal credit.

Jerry claims universal credit when he stops work because of cancer treatment. His girlfriend moves in to look after him. He does not realise he needs to tell the DWP. When he does tell the DWP some months later, he finds he has an overpayment of universal credit as they should have claimed as a couple.

Anna has an award of universal credit of £300 a month. One month, there is a mix-up in the system and two sums of £300 are paid into her bank account on the same day by mistake. Anna queries it and is told that this is an overpayment.

if you are overpaid because the DWP has treated you as a lone parent when, in fact, you have a partner living with you, it will work out how much was due to you as a couple and only recover the amount still remaining.

- **Decide whether to recover the overpayment.** By law, any overpayment is recoverable even if it is caused by an official error. However, the decision whether or not to recover the overpayment is at the decision maker's discretion. A code of practice will help decision makers decide whether they should exercise this discretion.

- **Decide from whom to recover the overpayment.** The general rule is that an overpayment can be recovered from the person to whom it was paid. If you claim jointly as a couple, it can be recovered from one or both of you, even if you are not the one who received the payment.

- **Decide how to recover the overpayment.** There are various methods the DWP can use to recover an overpayment.

What the law says

Recovering overpayments

- Universal credit is not recoverable unless the decision on your entitlement is changed – ie, it is revised or superseded by the DWP or changed by appeal.

- Regulations may give some exceptions to this rule.

- An overpayment is recoverable from the person who received the payment.

- Regulations may say that someone else is liable to repay the money, either instead or as well as the person who received the payment.

- Couples are both liable for any overpayment, regardless of which partner received the payment.

- Regulations will say how overpayments are calculated.

Section 105 Welfare Reform Act 2012

Do you have to pay back an overpayment?

The Department for Work and Pensions (DWP) is legally entitled to ask you to repay an overpayment, irrespective of what caused it, even if it was due to a DWP mistake. This means you cannot appeal against a decision to recover an overpayment.

However, the government has said that, in many cases, it does not intend to recover money if there has been an official error. There will be a code of practice for decision makers to follow to decide whether or not to ask you to repay an overpayment.

What the law says

Recovering overpayments

An overpayment is recoverable, even if the DWP caused it through official error.

Section 105 Welfare Reform Act 2012

What CPAG says

Recovering overpayments

CPAG is concerned that a system in which all overpayments of universal credit will be legally recoverable will be unfair on claimants, particularly if the overpayment has arisen through no fault of their own. A discretionary system to decide when to write off an overpayment is no substitute for an independent right of appeal. With more overpayments being recovered from claimants than would be allowed under the current system, more people will be left in hardship.

Although you cannot appeal against a decision to recover an overpayment, if you think you should not have to pay back the overpayment, you can dispute it. The code of practice will list the factors that should be taken into account to decide if an overpayment should not be recovered. You can use this to make your case.

Box A
What can you do if you have been overpaid?

- If paying back the overpayment will cause you hardship, you can ask for it to be written off. There should be details in the code of practice to help you make your case.

- If the DWP does not do as you ask, you can consider using the complaints procedure.

- If you are still unhappy, you can take your case to an Independent Case Examiner.

- You should check your award and if you disagree with the amount, you can ask for this to be 'revised' and then appeal if the DWP does not revise it. This is different from disputing the recovery of the overpayment. It is a way of making sure that the amount you are being asked to repay is correct and that your entitlement has been worked out correctly. You can do this at the same time as disputing recovery.

- In exceptional cases, you could seek advice about making a legal challenge, called a 'judicial review'.

EXAMPLE

Disputing an overpayment

Marion has separated from her partner, Geoff, who has moved out of the family home. The relationship has been off and on for a while and Marion hoped he would be back. She is currently feeling depressed and anxious. Six months later, Marion tells the DWP that Geoff has gone. The DWP revises her universal credit award from the date that Geoff moved out and works out how much she has been overpaid. She is told that this overpayment will be deducted each month from her award. Marion thinks this will leave her with insufficient money on which to manage. She does three things.

- She checks her award and discovers the date the DWP has said Geoff moved out is a month too early. She asks the DWP to revise the award. When it refuses, she appeals.

- She asks the DWP to write off the overpayment because the repayments are causing her hardship and her mental ill health makes it very hard for her to deal with problems, including reporting changes that affect her universal credit at the right time.

- She seeks advice from an advice centre. This helps her check that the amount of the overpayment is correct, and helps her with the dispute and appeal.

How do you pay back an overpayment?

The Department for Work and Pensions (DWP) can recover overpayments of universal credit by:

- making deductions from any ongoing award of benefit you have
- reducing any amount of arrears of benefit that are owed to you
- making deductions from your earnings
- taking court action against you

What the law says

How overpayments are recovered

- The DWP can recover an overpayment by:
  - making deductions from ongoing benefits or from arrears of benefits
  - making deductions from earnings
  - using the courts.

- If the DWP takes court action, it can recover court costs from you with the overpayment.

- There is no time limit on taking action, unless this is through the courts.

Sections 105 and 108 Welfare Reform Act 2012

The usual way of repaying an overpayment will be from your ongoing award of benefit. This might be universal credit or it might be another benefit. Regulations will say whether any benefits are excluded from this.

If you are employed, the DWP may be able to recover overpayments of universal credit from your earnings. Regulations will set out how the DWP can do this and these should include rules to ensure you are not left in hardship. The DWP will probably need to serve a notice on your employer, who will then be obliged to make these deductions. Your employer will be able to make an administrative charge for doing so, which is likely to be up to £1 for each deduction.

The DWP will be able to recover overpayments of universal credit through the courts and might do so if it cannot recover in another way – eg, if you are not receiving any benefits and not working. Court costs can be added to the overpayment and treated as part of it. The usual time limit on taking court action will apply – ie, six years in England and Wales and 20 years in Scotland. There is no limit for recovering overpayments in other ways.

EXAMPLE

Repaying an overpayment

Mona has been getting universal credit as someone with limited capability for work, but starts a low-paid job. Her award is adjusted. A year later, the DWP decides it has miscalculated her entitlement since she started working. Her award is reassessed and the amount she has been overpaid is worked out. The decision maker decides to recover the overpayment and to do so from both her ongoing universal credit award and her earnings, as her current award is low and a reasonable rate of recovery from her earnings will not cause her hardship. Her employer makes the deductions the DWP has requested from Mona's wages, plus an extra £1 for administration.

---

3. What can you do if you disagree with a decision?

If you disagree with a decision about your universal credit, you can challenge it.

You may first have to ask the Department for Work and Pensions (DWP) to look at its decision again. This is normally by asking for a 'revision'. A decision maker can revise a decision if you ask for this within a month of the date the decision was sent to you. If it has been longer than a month, a decision can still be revised if there are special reasons to extend the time limit, or if it can be revised or 'superseded' (another legal way to change a decision) on particular grounds.

What the law says

Challenging a decision

- Existing benefits legislation is amended to include universal credit in the current rules for revisions, supersessions and appeals.

- Most decisions made by the DWP on behalf of the Secretary of State can be appealed.

- Regulations may say that before appealing a decision, you must first ask the DWP to consider revising it.

- Regulations may say that if you apply for an appeal before asking for a revision when this is required, your application for an appeal can be treated as a request for a revision.

Section 102, and Schedule 2 paragraph 45 Welfare Reform Act 2012

If the DWP refuses to revise the decision, or does revise it but you are still not happy, you can then appeal to an independent appeal tribunal. **Note:** you will not be able to appeal against a decision to recover an overpayment.

Regulations are expected to say that, in most circumstances, you can normally only appeal against a decision if you have first asked for a revision. An appeal is to the First-tier Tribunal which is independent of the DWP. There are strict time limits on appealing. You should appeal within one month of being sent the decision, although the time limits can be extended for special reasons.

What CPAG says

Appealing decisions

Introducing a new requirement for claimants to request a revision before being able to exercise their right of appeal will introduce further delays into an already lengthy process and potentially cause hardship. Some people with strong cases may be put off from properly exercising their appeal rights by having to go through an extra stage in the process.

EXAMPLE

Disagreeing with a decision

Ilona gets universal credit for herself and her child. She has mental health problems and has been getting an additional element in her award for being ill. At her next medical examination, she is assessed as not having limited capability for work. She receives a decision saying that her universal credit award will no longer include the additional element. Ilona believes she is too ill to work and wants to challenge this. She is not sure how to do so and contacts the DWP to say she wants to appeal. Because the rules say she must first ask for a revision, the DWP treats this as a request to consider revising the decision. After considering the decision, the DWP decides not to revise it. Ilona can now appeal. She makes her written appeal immediately so she does not miss the deadline, and seeks advice from her local advice centre to help make her case.

4. Making a complaint

If you disagree with a decision on your universal credit award or payment, you should first check if you can ask for this to be changed by using the 'revision' and appeal process. Box A outlines the action you can take if the Department for Work and Pensions (DWP) says you have been overpaid. If you are unhappy with the way your universal credit claim has been handled, you can make a complaint.

You may want to complain about:

- a delay in dealing with your claim
- poor administration in the DWP benefit office
- poor advice from the DWP
- poor administration or advice from the Work Programme provider helping you look for or prepare for work
- a poorly conducted DWP medical examination
- the way the system affects you

How do you complain about the Department for Work and Pensions?

If you are unhappy with the way your claim has been handled, you should first take this up with the person dealing with it or with the office manager. If this does not resolve the issue, the Department for Work and Pensions has a complaints procedure. The first step is to contact the district manager (the office dealing with your claim can tell you who the district manager is). Once you have gone through all the steps in the complaints procedure and you still remain unhappy with the response, you can then take your case further to the Independent Case Examiner. Alternatively, you can contact your MP and ask her/him to refer your complaint to the Ombudsman.

How do you complain about a Work Programme provider?

If you are unhappy with the service, advice or administration from a Work Programme provider, you should first contact the provider. If you are not satisfied with the response, the provider should tell you what steps to take next.

How do you complain about a medical examination?

Department for Work and Pensions medical examinations are conducted by ATOS Healthcare. To complain about the conduct of a medical examination or about the healthcare professional who carried it out, you should initially contact ATOS Healthcare. If you are not satisfied with the response, it should tell you what steps to take next.

How do you use your MP?

If you do not have a particular universal credit issue to resolve, but you are unhappy with the way the system affects you, you may wish to take this up with your local MP.

You can also take up a specific problem with your MP. Normally it is best to do this if you have already tried to resolve the problem directly with the Department for Work and Pensions but are still unsatisfied. In particular, it can be useful to ask your MP for help if there has been a delay in your claim being dealt with.

You can write or email your MP, or go to a local 'surgery' – ie, the regular sessions that MPs usually have to meet their constituents. To find out who your MP is and how to contact her/him, see http://findyourmp.parliament.uk. You can also find contact details in your local library or town hall, or you can write to your local MP at the House of Commons, London SW1A 0AA.

Further information

ATOS Healthcare Customer Relations
Wing G, Government Buildings
Lawnswood
Leeds LS16 5PU
Tel: 0113 230 9175
email: customer-relations@atoshealthcare.com

The Parliamentary and Health Service Ombudsman
Millbank Tower
Millbank
London SW1P 4QP
Tel: 0345 015 4033
www.ombudsman.org.uk

Independent Case Examiner
Jupiter Drive
Chester CH70 8DR
Tel: 0845 606 0777
Textphone: 0151 801 8888
Fax 0151 801 8825
email: ice@dwp.gsi.gov.uk
www.ind-case-exam.org.uk

Chapter 8
Universal credit and other benefits

This chapter covers:

1. Means-tested working-age benefits and tax credits

2. Pension credit

3. Contribution-based jobseeker's allowance and contributory employment and support allowance

4. Bereavement benefits

5. Disability living allowance

6. Carer's allowance

7. Social fund payments

8. Other benefits and payments

9. Universal credit and other financial help

What you need to know

- Universal credit cannot be claimed at the same time as the means-tested benefits and tax credits it is replacing.

- Other benefits that are not being replaced by universal credit must be claimed separately. These are paid at the same time as universal credit.

- Entitlement to some other benefits means that a higher rate of universal credit is payable. It also affects your 'work-related requirements'. Some benefits count as income for universal credit and reduce the amount of universal credit that you get.

- Universal credit does not replace pension credit. However, if one partner in a couple is of working age, the couple must claim universal credit.

- Some social fund payments are being abolished, while others are being extended to people on universal credit.

- Receiving universal credit may mean you can get other financial help, such as health benefits, free school lunches for your children and Healthy Start vouchers.

1. Means-tested working-age benefits and tax credits

Which benefits and tax credits are being replaced by universal credit?

'Means-tested' benefits are based on the amount of income and capital you have. The following means-tested benefits will be abolished and will be replaced by universal credit for new claimants from October 2013:

- income support
- income-based jobseeker's allowance
- income-related employment and support allowance
- housing benefit

No new claims for these benefits will be accepted after October 2013. However, housing benefit will be phased out by April 2014, so new claims may still be possible if you are already entitled to another benefit or tax credit after this date.

Tax credits are assessed and paid based on your income during a complete tax year. Child tax credit and working tax credit will be abolished and will be replaced by universal credit for new claimants from 6 April 2014.

No new claims for tax credits will be accepted after 6 April 2014. However, is not clear in what circumstances you might be able to make a new claim for tax credits between October 2013 and 6 April 2014; it may be only if you claimed tax credits earlier in the 2013/14 tax year.

You cannot get any of the above benefits or tax credits at the same time as universal credit. If your partner is claiming one of these benefits or tax credits, you cannot get universal credit at the same time. If you are already getting one of these benefits or tax credits when universal credit is introduced in October 2013, you will be transferred onto universal credit at a later date. This process is not expected to be completed until October 2017.

What about council tax benefit?

Council tax benefit is a 'means-tested' benefit designed to help reduce your council tax bill. The rules are set by central government, but it is administered by local authorities.

The government intends to abolish council tax benefit by April 2013. However, unlike the other benefits that are being abolished, it will not be replaced by universal credit, and there is no additional amount in universal credit to help you pay your council tax. Instead, local authorities in England and the Scottish and Welsh governments will be given flexibility to set up their own versions of council tax benefit.

2. Pension credit

Pension credit is a 'means-tested' benefit for older people, based on the amount of income and capital you have. It can include additional amounts for carers, for severely disabled people and for mortgage interest. The qualifying age for pension credit is the same for men and women, but is based on women's retirement age, which is gradually increasing and will be 61 years and nine months in October 2013 when universal credit is introduced.

What the law says

Pension credit

- Regulations will introduce a housing element in pension credit.

- Regulations will introduce a savings limit for pension credit, to apply at least to the new housing element.

- Regulations will amend the rules on carers to remove the direct link with carer's allowance.

- Couples must claim universal credit, unless both have reached the qualifying age for pension credit.

Sections 34, 74 and 75, and Schedule 4 Part 1 Welfare Reform Act 2012

Can you still claim pension credit?

Pension credit is not being replaced by universal credit, which is only for people of working age. You will still be able to claim pension credit if you are single and have reached the pension credit qualifying age, or are a member of a couple and both of you have reached the qualifying age. You will not be able to make a new claim for pension credit if your partner has not reached the qualifying age. If you are already getting pension credit at the time universal credit is introduced, the government intends that you will continue to get it, even if your partner has not reached the qualifying age.

Can you get pension credit as well as universal credit?

You cannot claim pension credit at the same time as universal credit. You will be entitled to one or the other, but will not have a choice about which one you claim.

What other changes are there?

The pension credit rules will be changed to include amounts for rent and for children. These will replace housing benefit and child tax credit, which are being abolished. No new claims for tax credits will be allowed from April 2014, so the new amount for children will have to be available as part of pension credit by this date. Housing benefit for people over the qualifying age for pension credit will remain until October 2014, when it will be replaced by a new housing element in pension credit. The government also intends to introduce a savings limit for pension credit (to be applied to the new housing element) to maintain the current position. If a savings limit is applied more widely, the government has said that this will be substantially higher than the current limit in housing benefit (£16,000). The rules for carers will be simplified with a new definition of caring responsibilities, which is intended to cover, but not be limited to, people entitled to carer's allowance.

EXAMPLE

Pension credit

Catriona and Patrick are a couple. Catriona is 47 and Patrick is 61 when universal credit is introduced. When Patrick reaches the qualifying age for pension credit a few months later, he cannot claim pension credit. They must claim universal credit as a couple, but only Catriona is subject to the work-related requirements.

3. Contribution-based jobseeker's allowance and contributory employment and support allowance

'Contributory' benefits are based on the national insurance contributions you have paid or been credited with from your earnings. In your working life, you may currently get the following benefits.

- You may get **contribution-based jobseeker's allowance** for six months if you meet the national insurance contribution conditions and you are 'available for and actively seeking work'. The amount you get is reduced by any earnings over £5 a week and any pension payments over £50 a week that you have.

- You may get **contributory employment and support allowance** if you meet the national insurance contribution conditions and have 'limited capability for work' because of illness or disability. From April 2012, payment of this is limited to one year, unless you are assessed as being in the 'support group' for the most severely disabled people. The amount you get is reduced by 50 per cent of any pension payments over £85 a week. It can continue to be paid in full if you are earning less than £20 a week (or £97.50 under special rules about certain kinds of work).

What the law says

Jobseeker's allowance and employment and support allowance

- Regulations will deal with the situation where someone is entitled to universal credit and to either contribution-based jobseeker's allowance or contributory employment and support allowance at the same time (known as 'dual entitlement'). These may say that, in certain cases, only universal credit is payable.

- In cases of dual entitlement, regulations may say that the work-related requirements and sanctions apply to both benefits. They will also ensure that if your contributory benefit is reduced or stopped because of a sanction, this will not lead to an increase in universal credit.

Schedule 5 Welfare Reform Act 2012

Can you still claim contributory benefits?

After the introduction of universal credit, you will still be able to claim contribution-based jobseeker's allowance or contributory employment and support allowance. If you cannot get universal credit because, for example, your savings are too high, you will still be able to claim one of these benefits, usually for a limited time.

Can you get contributory benefits as well as universal credit?

You may be entitled to contribution-based jobseeker's allowance or contributory employment and support allowance at the same time as universal credit, but you will not receive both in full. This could mean you get the contributory benefit. However, because it counts as income for universal credit, it reduces your entitlement, leaving you with a top-up of universal credit. However, regulations may say that, in certain cases, the contributory benefit will not be paid at all and payment will be made entirely by universal credit instead.

What other changes are there?

If you are entitled to a contributory benefit and universal credit, or you move from one to another, the rules on 'work-related requirements', 'sanctions' and 'hardship payments' will apply to both benefits. The earnings rules in contribution-based jobseeker's allowance and contributory employment and support allowance may be amended to be simplified and aligned with the universal credit earnings disregards and withdrawal rate.

EXAMPLE

Contribution-based jobseeker's allowance and contributory employment and support allowance

Tony has been working for several years when he falls ill. He has £30,000 in savings. He cannot get universal credit because he has too much capital. He is entitled to employment and support allowance, based on his national insurance contributions, and is placed in the work-related activity group. Under current government plans, he can only get employment and support allowance for one year.

4. Bereavement benefits

Bereavement benefits are based on the national insurance contributions made by your late spouse or civil partner. If your spouse or civil partner dies and you are under pension age, you may be able to get the following benefits.

- You may get **bereavement allowance** for one year if your late spouse or civil partner met the national insurance contribution conditions. It is not affected by your other income.

- You may get **widowed parent's allowance** if your late spouse or civil partner met the national insurance contributions conditions and you are responsible for a child or young person. It is not affected by your other income.

- You may get a one-off **lump-sum bereavement payment** if your late spouse or civil partner met the national insurance contribution conditions. It is not affected by your other income.

Can you still claim bereavement benefits?

After the introduction of universal credit, you will still be able to claim bereavement benefits. The government has said that bereavement benefits are not suitable for replacement by universal credit.

Can you get bereavement benefits as well as universal credit?

You may be entitled to a bereavement benefit at the same time as universal credit, but you cannot get both in full. It is likely that you will receive the bereavement allowance or widowed parent's allowance in full, but your universal credit will be reduced. Bereavement benefits will generally count as income for universal credit, but may be partially ignored to ensure that widows and widowers are not worse off than under the current system. In some cases, the amount of your bereavement benefit may mean that you do not qualify for universal credit at all.

What other changes are there?

The government is currently reviewing bereavement benefits and published options for consultation in December 2011. The proposals seek to simplify the system by combining the three separate payments into one benefit, and reinforce the view that national insurance contributions provide short-term protection only. The options include increasing the lump-sum grant available and drastically cutting the length of time payments are made to bereaved parents with children to only one year.

EXAMPLE

Bereavement benefits

Bianca's husband dies suddenly. He was the main earner and had been working for several years. She is left with two children, a mortgage and no savings. She is entitled to widowed parent's allowance, but this is not sufficient for her to live on. She can get a top-up of universal credit for the children and some help with the mortgage interest, possibly after a waiting period.

---

5. Disability living allowance

Disability living allowance is a 'non-means-tested', 'non-contributory' benefit to help towards the extra costs of disability. It does not depend on your income and capital, nor on whether or not you have paid sufficient national insurance contributions. It is currently disregarded as income when 'means-tested' benefits and tax credits are calculated. Receipt of disability living allowance for an adult or child can lead to additional payments in the current means-tested benefits and tax credits.

What the law says

Disability living allowance

- Disability living allowance for adults will be abolished and replaced with a new personal independence payment for people of working age.

- The personal independence payment includes a daily living component and a mobility component, both payable at two rates.

Sections 77-95 Welfare Reform Act 2012

Can you still claim disability living allowance?

The government intends to abolish disability living allowance for adults and replace it with a personal independence payment from April 2013. If you are making a new claim from that date, you will claim personal independence payment. If you are already getting disability living allowance, you will be reassessed for personal independence payment, but this process may take several years.

You will still be able to claim disability living allowance for a disabled child, as this is not part of the planned reforms.

Can you get disability living allowance as well as as universal credit?

You will be able to get disability living allowance or personal independence payment and universal credit in full. Disability living allowance and personal independence payment will be ignored as income for universal credit. When universal credit is introduced, there will be a period of overlap, during which time some people will get disability living allowance and some will get personal independence payment.

If you are a working-age adult, there is nothing to suggest that your disability living allowance or personal independence payment will mean you are entitled to more universal credit. Additional amounts for disabled adults in universal credit are linked to whether you have 'limited capability for work' or 'limited capability for work-related activity', as currently used for employment and support allowance. This assessment will also determine the 'conditionality group' in which you are placed for universal credit, not receipt of disability living allowance or personal independence payment.

However, the government has said that disabled people in work will qualify for a higher earnings disregard, so it is possible that this may be linked to receipt of disability living allowance or personal independence payment.

Disability living allowance will not be abolished for children under 16. There will be additional payments for disabled children in universal credit, which will remain linked to receipt of disability living allowance. There will be a higher rate addition for the most severely disabled children getting the highest rate of the care component.

EXAMPLE

Disability living allowance

Tina gets the lowest rate care component and the lower rate mobility component of disability living allowance. She rents her flat and is single. Tina is made redundant and she claims universal credit. She is assessed as not having limited capability for work. She gets universal credit, which includes a standard allowance for herself and an amount for her rent. It does not include an addition for her disability. She is expected to look for work.

6. Carer's allowance

Carer's allowance is a 'non-means-tested', 'non-contributory' benefit for carers looking after a severely disabled person. It does not depend on your income and capital, nor on whether you have paid sufficient national insurance contributions. It counts as income for 'means-tested' benefits, but entitlement to carer's allowance means you get an additional carer premium paid in any means-tested benefit. Entitlement to carer's allowance depends on the cared-for person getting the middle or highest rate care component of disability living allowance. If you are a carer and getting carer's allowance, you are not required to be 'actively seeking work'. It is currently possible to do some part-time work (earning less than £100 a week) and continue to receive carer's allowance in full.

Can you still claim carer's allowance?

After the introduction of universal credit, you will still be able to claim carer's allowance, but it is likely to be reformed in order to be integrated into the new system.

Can you get carer's allowance as well as universal credit?

You will be able to get carer's allowance at the same time as universal credit, but you will not be able to receive both in full because carer's allowance will count as income for universal credit and will reduce the amount of universal credit you get. Getting carer's allowance will probably mean that you are entitled to an additional amount for being a carer in your universal credit. It will also probably mean that you are treated as a carer and will not have any 'work-related requirements'.

What other changes are there?

The government believes that carer's allowance is ineffective and confusing, and is considering making changes to it. It has said that the earnings rules will be amended to provide support and improve opportunities to work. There will also be changes to the qualifying conditions to integrate it into the new personal independence payment and this may involve a new way of defining caring responsibilities.

> ### EXAMPLE
>
> #### Carer's allowance
>
> Sami gets carer's allowance for looking after his partner Lauren, who gets disability living allowance care component paid at the middle rate and has limited capability for work. They get universal credit that includes a carer's addition and an addition for limited capability for work. Sami has no work-related requirements – ie, he is not expected to do anything to get full benefit. Lauren has to attend work-focused interviews and prepare for work.

7. Social fund payments

The social fund is a system of additional payments to help people on low incomes meet exceptional costs. There are various payments.

- **Community care grants** are discretionary amounts paid to help vulnerable people on benefits return to or remain in the community.

- **Crisis loans** are repayable payments to help with essential costs or living expenses in an emergency.

- **Budgeting loans** are repayable discretionary amounts, payable to people who have been on certain benefits for at least six months.

- **Sure Start maternity grants** are grants of £500 to help with the cost of a newborn baby. They are for people on a low income who have no other child under the age of 16 in the household.

- **Funeral payments** are grants to help with the costs of a funeral for people on a low income.

- **Cold weather payments** are payments of £25 a week when there are seven consecutive days of freezing weather. They are for people on a low income who have a disability or young children.

What the law says

Social fund payments

- Community care grants and crisis loans will be abolished and replaced by locally administered assistance provided by local authorities in England and the Scottish and Welsh governments.

- Budgeting loans will be abolished and replaced by payments on account of universal credit for people in need. Before they are abolished, they will be extended to cover maternity or funeral expenses, which are currently excluded.

- Social fund loans can be recovered from your earnings.

- The current qualifying benefits for the social fund will be abolished.

Sections 33, 70, 71 and 106 Welfare Reform Act 2012

The social fund will be reformed, and all the above payments will be affected by the introduction of universal credit.

- **Community care grants** and **crisis loans** will be abolished from April 2013. English local authorities and the Scottish and Welsh governments will decide on an alternative way of meeting the needs of vulnerable people or in emergencies. The criteria may vary from one area to another.

- **Budgeting loans** will be abolished and replaced by advance payments of universal credit, known as 'payments on account', from October 2013. There is more information on these payments in Chapter 3. The amount you get may depend on what you need it for, what other money is available to you or on how long you have been getting universal credit. You will have to repay the loan by deductions from your ongoing universal credit payments. Deductions may also be made from your earnings.

- **Sure Start maternity grants** will be paid automatically to people getting universal credit when the criteria are met. You should not have to make a separate claim, but there will have to be a process for notifying and confirming pregnancy, which currently involves the signature of a health professional. A maternity grant can be claimed from 15 weeks before the date your baby is due, up to three months after the birth.

- **Cold weather payments** will be paid automatically to people on universal credit when the criteria are met. This is similar to the current situation, in which there is no need to claim and payments are made automatically when the temperature at your local weather station is recorded as sufficiently low.

- **Funeral payments** will be outside the universal credit system and will continue to be made by the Department for Work and Pensions. The government has said that entitlement will be extended to people on universal credit.

8. Other benefits and payments

The government has said that other benefits will remain outside universal credit, including:

- child benefit
- statutory sick pay
- statutory maternity, paternity and adoption pay
- maternity allowance
- industrial injuries benefits

There is a full list of benefits that will remain in Chapter 1.

You will be able to claim these benefits after the introduction of universal credit. It is expected that you will be able to receive them at the same time as universal credit, but you may not get both in full. However, the interaction of these benefits with universal credit is not yet clear. Under the current system, these payments are treated differently for benefits and tax credits. Rules on income and earnings may be changed so that these payments are better integrated with universal credit.

What about other work-related payments?

The government has indicated that other work-related payments may not be needed under universal credit. This may include:

- in-work credit for lone parents
- return-to-work credit for disabled people
- job grant

There is no bonus payment in universal credit for starting work as there is in the current benefits system.

9. Universal credit and other financial help

Under the current benefits and tax credits system, if you get income-related benefits, such as income support, income-based jobseeker's allowance, income-related employment and support allowance, pension credit or child tax credit, you can qualify for other financial help. This is known as 'passporting'. Other financial help includes:

- free prescriptions
- free NHS sight tests and glasses
- dental treatment
- fares to hospital
- Healthy Start vouchers
- free school lunches
- school clothing grants
- Warm Front or Energy Assistance Scheme help
- legal aid
- local leisure facility discounts
- social tariffs from utility companies

Some schemes are administered by central government departments, some by the Scottish and Welsh governments, and some by local authorities. Some of this passported help is provided in cash or vouchers and some by discounts on charges. In general, you must make a separate claim for the passported help. In some cases, you must receive the necessary out-of-work benefit to qualify and people not getting the required benefit but who are on a low income are excluded. When universal credit is introduced and these benefits are abolished, the current criteria will no longer exist.

What the law says

Passported benefits

Some universal credit claimants are entitled to other benefits, such as free school meals.

Schedule 2 Welfare Reform Act 2012

The government is currently considering:

- replacing passported benefits with an additional cash amount in universal credit
- keeping passported benefits as benefits in cash, vouchers or discounts, linked to the receipt of universal credit within a certain level of income
- withdrawing passported benefits gradually, rather than an abrupt 'cliff edge' when all are lost at a certain level of income

Further information

There is more information about the rules for current benefits and tax credits in CPAG's *Welfare Benefits and Tax Credits Handbook*.

Chapter 9
Universal credit and specific groups of people

This chapter highlights the impact of universal credit on the following groups of people:

1. Lone parents

2. Carers

3. Disabled people

4. Older people

5. People from abroad

What you need to know

- The 'work-related requirements' that lone parents must meet to get universal credit vary, depending on the age of their youngest child.

- Carers have no work-related requirements and may be entitled to an additional amount of universal credit.

- Disabled people must have a medical assessment of their ability to work or to prepare for work. They may have no work-related requirements, or some or all requirements, depending on the extent of their disability. Some may qualify for an additional amount.

- People over the qualifying age for pension credit cannot claim universal credit and must still claim pension credit. If one member of a couple reaches the qualifying age for pension credit and the other is of working age, they must claim universal credit.

- Certain people from abroad are excluded from universal credit.

1. Lone parents

Can lone parents claim universal credit?

Lone parents will be able to claim universal credit.

As in the current system of tax credits, if you are a lone parent you will make a single claim for universal credit, but a joint claim as a couple if you have a partner living with you. It is important to be clear about whether you are a lone parent and be aware that if a partner moves in with you, even if s/he is not the parent of your child, you become a couple and will have a joint universal credit award.

What the law says

Lone parents

- You make a single claim for universal credit if you are a lone parent, a joint claim if you are in a couple.

- If you are a lone parent, your work-related requirements depend on the age of your youngest child. If your child is under one, you have no work-related requirements.

- If your child is under five, you must attend work-focused interviews.

- If your child is aged three or four, you may have to show that you are preparing for work. The government intends there to be some flexibility so you may be required to prepare for being a jobseeker once your child reaches five.

- If your child is aged five and over, you must meet all the work-related requirements. You should be allowed to restrict your availability to some extent and be allowed a reasonable amount of time to arrange childcare before starting work.

Sections 19-22 Welfare Reform Act 2012

Are there any special rules for lone parents?

If you are a lone parent, the maximum amount of universal credit payable to you will be based on an allowance for yourself and your children, plus an amount for housing costs and, if you are in work, an amount for childcare costs. There are additional amounts if you care for a disabled child or adult, or if you or your child are disabled.

There is no mention of an additional amount specifically for lone parents, but there are special rules that allow lone parents to keep more of their earnings.

There is more information on how universal credit is calculated in Chapter 4.

Lone parents on universal credit will have different 'work-related requirements', depending on the age of their youngest child. Lone parents will be required to be 'available for and actively seeking work' once their youngest child has reached five. However, the government has also referred to 'school age' and assumes that a lone parent will be available for work once her/his child has actually started school, which should take into account regional differences.

If you do not comply with your work-related requirements, your universal credit may be 'sanctioned' and you will receive a reduced amount. If you are sanctioned, 'hardship payments' may be available. There are exceptions for people who have recently been a victim of domestic violence. If this applies to you, the work-related requirements should not be imposed on you for 13 weeks.

There is more information about sanctions in Chapter 6.

A crucial consideration for most lone parents when contemplating taking up work is childcare. The government has said that childcare support will be extended under universal credit. There will be no minimum number of hours you must work to qualify for help with childcare; any work will qualify. Universal credit may therefore include an amount to help with childcare costs if you are working and paying a registered childcare provider – eg, a childminder, nursery or after-school club. The full costs of your childcare are not covered – only 70 per cent of the costs, up to an overall limit, as in the current tax credits sytem. The limits will be £760 a month for one child or £1,300 for two or more children, so the most you will get will be £532 or £910 a month (70 per cent).

What about other benefits for lone parents?

Child benefit will remain outside universal credit. You will be able to claim child benefit as well as universal credit.

Lone parents who have been bereaved will still be able to claim widowed parent's allowance.

The Sure Start maternity grant and Healthy Start vouchers are not being abolished, but their qualifying conditions may be linked to receipt of universal credit.

2. Carers

Can carers claim universal credit?

Carers looking after a severely disabled person will be able to claim universal credit.

What the law says

Carers

• Universal credit includes an additional amount for certain carers.

• Certain carers do not have any work-related requirements.

Sections 12 and 19 Welfare Reform Act 2012

Are there any special rules for carers?

There will be an additional amount in universal credit for people who have regular and substantial caring responsibilities for a severely disabled person. The government has said that you will get this if you provide care for at least 35 hours a week. The government has not yet said how much the carer's addition will be.

The carer's addition will not be payable at the same time as a 'limited capability for work' or 'limited capability for work-related activity' addition for yourself if you are also disabled. However, if you are in a couple, you can get a carer's addition for yourself and a limited capability for work or limited capability for work-related activity addition for your disabled partner.

Box A

Foster carers

- Foster carers who are legally approved to look after a child or young person by arrangement with a local authority or voluntary organisation are treated differently from carers looking after a disabled person.

- There are special rules for foster carers in universal credit.

- Lone foster carers do not have any 'work-related requirements' until their youngest foster child reaches 16, when they will be required to look for and be available for work.

- In exceptional circumstances when a foster child who is 16 or 17 needs full-time care, the foster carer is only required to participate in 'work-focused interviews' until the child reaches 18 or the placement ends.

- Fostering couples are required to nominate a lead carer. The other member of the couple has all the work-related requirements, unless there are exceptional circumstances and the foster child needs full-time care by two adults.

- Fostering is not treated as being self-employed or in work.

- Fostering payments are not taken into account as earnings or income. There is no additional amount in universal credit for being a foster carer.

Carers who are in work will see their overall universal credit award reduced, in the same way as other claimants. There is no extra earnings disregard for carers. However, you will not lose the carer's addition in universal credit just because you are working (even if you earn more than the current £100 a week limit for carer's allowance), provided you are still caring for at least 35 hours a week.

Carers who spend at least 35 hours a week caring for a severely disabled person will not have any work-related requirements. The government has said that there will be flexibility, so that different work-related requirements may be applied to other carers depending on their circumstances.

What about other benefits for carers?

Carers will still be able to claim carer's allowance, but this is likely to be changed to align the qualifying conditions with the new personal independence payment and universal credit earnings rules.

There is more information about this in Chapter 8.

3. Disabled people

Can disabled people claim universal credit?

People with disabilities will be able to claim universal credit.

Are there any special rules for disabled people?

There will be special rules for some people with disabilities. These affect how much universal credit you will get, what kind of 'work-related requirements' you will have and, if you work, how much of your earnings you can keep before your universal credit is affected.

Universal credit will include additional amounts for disabled adults and children. These will be paid at two rates depending on the severity of the disability. For a child, this will depend on the amount of disability living allowance s/he gets, and will also be paid for children who are registered blind. For an adult, this will depend on a

What the law says

People with disabilities

- Universal credit includes an additional amount for people with limited capability for work.

- Universal credit includes an additional amount for people with limited capability for work-related activity.

- People with limited capability for work must prepare for work, which means they may be required to take part in certain activities, such as training or work experience.

- People with limited capability for work-related activity do not have any work-related requirements.

Sections 12, 19 and 21 Welfare Reform Act 2012

medical assessment of your 'limited capability for work', as is currently the case for employment and support allowance.

If you are disabled and you also care for someone who is disabled, you will not be able to get a limited capability for work or 'limited capability for work-related activity' addition and a carer's addition in your universal credit. However, if you are in a couple and you are disabled and your partner is a carer, you could get a limited capability for work or limited capability for work-related activity addition for yourself and a carer's addition for your partner.

There will be a higher 'earnings disregard' for disabled people and couples with either partner disabled. This is proposed to be £7,000 a year and is the amount you can earn before the amount of your universal credit is reduced. However, it is not clear how you will qualify for this disregard. It may be linked to the limited capability for work test. However, as it is not currently possible to be assessed as such while in full-time work, it is hoped that it will be extended to include receipt of other disability benefits.

What about other benefits for disabled people?

You will still be able to claim contributory employment and support allowance if you have worked and paid sufficient national insurance contributions, although payment will be limited to one year for most people.

Disability living allowance will be abolished for new claims from working-age claimants from April 2013 and replaced by personal independence payment. There is more information about this in Chapter 8.

It is likely that getting disability living allowance or personal independence payment will not qualify you for an additional amount in universal credit. However, the government has said that disabled people in work will qualify for a higher 'earnings disregard', so it is possible that this may be linked to receipt of disability living allowance or personal independence payment. Disability living allowance is not being abolished for children and will continue to be the main criteria for getting the disability addition for a disabled child.

4. Older people

Can older people claim universal credit?

Older people will not be able to claim universal credit.

- Single people over the qualifying age for pension credit will not be able to claim universal credit.

- Couples who are both over the qualifying age for pension credit will not be able to claim universal credit.

- A couple with one partner who has reached the qualifying age for pension credit and one under the qualifying age for pension credit will be able to claim universal credit, but will not be able to claim pension credit. They will not have a choice. Couples who are already on pension credit when universal credit is introduced will be allowed to remain on pension credit.

The qualifying age for pension credit for men and women will be around 61 years and nine months in October 2013, when universal credit is introduced.

What the law says

Older people

- One of the basic conditions of universal credit is that you have not reached the qualifying age for pension credit.

- In future, both claimants in a couple must have reached pension age in order to claim pension credit.

Section 4, and Schedule 2 paragraph 64 Welfare Reform Act 2012

Are there any special rules for older people?

If a couple is claiming universal credit, only the working-age partner will have 'work-related requirements'.

What CPAG says

Older people

Older people's organisations have argued that a special rule is needed to ensure that couples with one partner over the qualifying age for pension credit and one of working age are not hugely disadvantaged under universal credit. If you reach the qualifying age for pension credit just before universal credit is introduced, you will be entitled to around £217.90 pension credit a week, regardless of your partner's age. However, if you reach the qualifying age after October 2013, you stay on universal credit, which will have a couple rate of around £111.45 a week, until your partner also reaches the qualifying age. This seems very unfair. It has also been pointed out that a single person over the qualifying age for pension credit will be entitled to around £142.70 a week pension credit, so couples will be in the unfortunate position of being financially better off if they separate. The government has given no assurance that there will be any additional 'pensioner' amount in universal credit.

What about other benefits for older people?

Universal credit does not replace pension credit or retirement pension. Pension credit will include additional amounts for rent and probably also for children, following the abolition of housing benefit and child tax credit.

Separate plans suggest that the basic levels of pension credit and state retirement pension may be replaced in future by a flat-rate pension for everyone.

5. People from abroad

Can people from abroad claim universal credit?

People who have come to live in the UK from other countries will be able to claim universal credit if they have certain types of permission to live in the UK, but some groups will be excluded.

What the law says

People from abroad

- One of the basic conditions is that the claimant must be in Great Britain.

- Regulations will set out circumstances in which a person is treated as being, or not being, in Great Britain.

- People subject to immigration control are excluded from universal credit.

Section 4, and Schedule 2 paragraph 54 Welfare Reform Act 2012

You will be excluded from universal credit if your entry clearance to the UK says that you must have 'no recourse to public funds'. This is usually stamped in your passport if you are from outside the European Economic Area and you are in the UK as a student, visitor or with a work visa. Universal credit will be added to the list of what counts as 'public funds' in the Immigration Rules.

You will be excluded from universal credit if you are an asylum seeker. You are an asylum seeker if you are waiting for a decision from the Home Office on an application for refugee status in the UK, or if you are appealing against a negative decision. The current asylum support system will remain outside universal credit.

Are there any special rules for people from abroad?

There is no specific mention of the current presence and residence tests, but it is likely that universal credit will mirror the current rules for means-tested benefits and tax credits.

- You may be excluded from universal credit if you are not 'habitually resident' in the UK. This includes being settled in the UK for an appreciable period, and also applies to British citizens returning to the UK from living abroad.

- You may be excluded from universal credit if you do not have the 'right to reside' in the UK. This particularly affects you if you are a national of a European Economic Area country. You are generally required to show a link to the labour market as a worker, self-employed person, jobseeker or family member.

What about other benefits for people from abroad?

There are special rules for certain groups of people from abroad for most of the benefits that will remain. The rules for contribution-based jobseeker's allowance, contributory employment and support allowance, and statutory maternity, paternity and adoption pay are being changed so that only those who are entitled to work in the UK will be able to claim.

Appendix 1

Glossary of terms

Actively seeking work
Looking for paid work. A person must normally spend the same number of hours a week looking for work as the Department for Work and Pensions expects her/him to work.

Appointee
Someone, usually a relative, who is authorised by the Department for Work and Pensions to claim benefit on another person's behalf if that person cannot claim for her/himself – eg, perhaps because of a learning disability.

Available for work
Willing and able to take up work. This normally means full-time work, but may be restricted if the Department for Work and Pensions agrees it is reasonable.

Benefit cap
The maximum amount of social security benefits that someone can receive. This includes most benefits, but there are some exceptions and some groups to whom the cap does not apply.

Capital
This includes savings, investments, certain lump-sum payments and property which is not a person's home.

Civil penalty
A fine that can be imposed if someone is overpaid a benefit because s/he failed to provide information or gave incorrect information, and is not being prosecuted for fraud or another benefit offence.

Claimant commitment
A document setting out what someone must do while claiming universal credit, and the possible penalties if its terms are not met.

Conditionality
Being required to undertake certain activities, usually focused on moving towards work, in order to continue to receive benefit.

Conditionality group
The level and type of work-related requirements that are imposed on someone when s/he claims universal credit.

Conditionality threshold
The amount of a person's earnings (or joint earnings for couples) above which s/he is not expected to look for more work.

Contributory benefit
A benefit for which entitlement depends on having paid a certain amount of national insurance contributions.

Couple
A man and a woman (or two people of the same sex) living together who are married or civil partners, or who are living together as if they were married or civil partners.

Disregard floor
The minimum amount of earnings that are disregarded when working out the amount of universal credit for someone who has housing costs.

Earnings disregard
The amount of a person's wages or income from self-employment that can be kept before her/his universal credit starts being reduced. The amount depends on personal circumstances.

Elements
Amounts for children, disabilities, caring responsibilities, housing and childcare which make up part of a person's maximum universal credit award.

European Economic Area
The 27 European Union member states, plus Iceland, Norway and Liechtenstein. For benefit purposes, Switzerland is also treated as part of the European Economic Area.

Habitually resident
Someone who has a settled intention to stay in the UK, and who has usually been living here for a period.

Hardship payments
Payments of universal credit made if someone's entitlement has been reduced by a sanction and s/he faces financial hardship.

Independent Case Examiner
A body handling complaints against agencies within the Department for Work and Pensions.

Jobseeker's agreement
A document setting out what a person must do to look for work in order to claim jobseeker's allowance. To be replaced by the claimant commitment.

Judicial review
A way of challenging the decisions of government departments, local authorities and some tribunals against which there is no right of appeal.

Limited capability for work
A test of whether a person's ability to work is limited by a health condition.

Limited capability for work-related activity
A test of how severe a person's health problems are and whether her/his ability to prepare for work is limited.

Means-tested benefit
A benefit that is only paid if someone's income and capital are low enough.

National minimum wage
A set minimum hourly rate that employers must pay.

No recourse to public funds
A restriction that applies to people subject to immigration control as part of their entry conditions to the UK, prohibiting them from claiming most benefits and tax credits, including universal credit.

Non-contributory benefit
A benefit, for which entitlement does not depend on having paid a certain amount of national insurance contributions.

Non-means-tested benefit
A benefit that is paid regardless of the amount of someone's income or capital.

Overpayment
An amount of benefit that is paid which is more than a person's entitlement.

Passporting
A term used to describe when entitlement to a particular benefit allows access to other benefits or sources of help.

Payment exceptions service
A discretionary system to make more regular payments of universal credit for people in exceptional circumstances who cannot manage monthly payments.

Payment on account
An advance of universal credit, paid if there is a delay in deciding someone's claim or in cases of financial need.

Penalty as an alternative to prosecution
A type of fine that can be offered to someone instead of being prosecuted, if the Department for Work and Pensions thinks an offence may have been committed.

Permitted work
Work which a person with limited capability for work can still do while claiming benefit.

Person subject to immigration control
Someone who requires leave to enter or remain in the UK but does not have it, or who has leave to remain but is prohibited from having recourse to public funds, or has leave to remain in the UK on the basis of a sponsorship agreement.

Personal adviser
A person whose job is to discuss your work-related requirements. S/he may be an employee of the Department for Work and Pensions, or someone contracted to provide services under the Work Programme.

Qualifying age for pension credit
Linked to women's pension age, which is currently increasing from age 60, will equalise with men's pension age in 2018, and will reach 66 in 2020.

Real-time information system
A new system, where employers send HM Revenue and Customs information about your earnings every time you are paid, which is then used by the Department for Work and Pensions to adjust your universal credit award.

Responsible carer
The person in a couple who spends the most time looking after the children.

Revision
A statutory method that allows benefit decisions to be changed.

Right to reside
A social security test, mainly affecting European Economic Area nationals, which must be satisfied in order to claim certain benefits.

Sanction
A reduction in a person's universal credit award for failing to meet her/his work-related requirements without a good reason. The term is also used if a person's universal credit is stopped for a set length of time because s/he has committed an offence.

Standard allowance
The basic amount of universal credit paid for a single adult or a couple.

Supersession
A statutory method which allows benefit decisions to be changed, usually as a result of a change in circumstances.

Taper
The rate at which a person's maximum universal credit will reduce as her/his earnings increase.

Transitional protection
A way of making sure that a person transferring to universal credit from another benefit will not receive less money on universal credit than s/he did before.

Waiting period
The time you must wait at the start of your claim before payment can start, or before payment of housing costs can start.

Work preparation
The activities that someone with a health condition may have to undertake to prepare for work.

Work-focused interview
An interview to discuss future work opportunities and the barriers that may prevent someone from working.

Work-focused health-related assessment
An assessment of the barriers to working caused by a person's health problems or disability, which may have to be carried out if s/he is required to prepare for work.

Work-related activity group
The group into which people who pass the test of limited capability for work but not the test of limited capability for work-related activity (ie, those with less severe disabilities or illnesses) are placed.

Work-related requirements
The activities that a person must undertake to continue to receive the full amount of universal credit.

Appendix 2

Universal credit legislation
Welfare Reform Act 2012

Sources of information
Welfare Reform Bill Explanatory Notes

Welfare Reform Bill: committee stage report, Research Paper 11/48, House of Commons Library, 8 June 2011

Welfare Reform Bill: universal credit provisions, Research Paper 11/24, House of Commons Library, 7 March 2011

Department for Work and Pensions, *Universal Credit: welfare that works*, Cm 7957, November 2010

Department for Work and Pensions, Universal Credit Policy Briefing Notes series, March–November 2011

Department for Work and Pensions, *Impact Assessments*, February–November 2011

Department for Work and Pensions, *Equality Impact Assessments*, March–November 2011

House of Commons Public Bill Committee on the Welfare Reform Bill 2010-11, Reports of Proceedings, March–May 2011

You can find these and other documents on

the DWP's website at www.dwp.gov.uk/policy/welfare-reform and/or the UK Parliament website at http://services.parliament.uk/bills/2010-11/welfarereform.html

Index